SELECTIONS FROM THE FEDERALIST

EDITED, WITH AN INTRODUCTION

BY

WILLIAM BENNETT MUNRO
PROFESSOR OF MUNICIPAL GOVERNMENT
IN HARVARD UNIVERSITY

CAMBRIDGE
HARVARD UNIVERSITY PRESS
1914

PREFACE

Too little use has been made of *The Federalist* as a means of affording instruction both in the foundations of American government and in the principles of English composition. In clearness both of thought and expression these letters of Alexander Hamilton, James Madison, and John Jay are not surpassed in the whole range of American political literature. In order that some of them may be more conveniently used in the training of young men for clear-headed citizenship, this volume of selections has been arranged.

For several years the editor has been using *The Federalist* in his class-room. Students have made their approach to the study of federal government through its pages. On the whole the results have been very satisfactory, although some of the letters have proved much better than others as starting-points for class-room discussion. In determining what should go into the present volume and what should not, this experience has been the sole guide. It happens, however, that all the selections have come from among the first fifty of the original letters.

The text of *The Federalist* from which these selections have been taken is that of the first collected edition, published by McLean (New York, 1788). It differs only in some minor matters of form from the texts of the original letters printed in the newspapers of that year and the year before, and is said to have received the benefit of Madison's revision in preparation for the press. The importance of using the original text is obvious in the case of articles written for such a special and immediate purpose; yet most editors have followed either the revised text of 1802, or the amended " original text " which Dawson prepared for his edition of 1863. The only foot-notes included in the present *Selections* are those which appeared in the edition of 1788, and which were put there by the authors themselves.

W.B.M.

CAMBRIDGE, December 28, 1913.

CONTENTS

SELECTIONS FROM THE FEDERALIST

INTRODUCTION

I. THE MAKING OF THE CONSTITUTION

In the early summer of 1787 a group of fifty-five men, representing all the states except Rhode Island, met in Philadelphia to work out some plan of union which would better serve their common interests than the one provided by the Articles of Confederation. These Articles had been adopted in 1777 by the delegates of the various states in the Continental Congress, and this action was subsequently ratified by the states themselves. But the Confederation which was thereby established amounted to little more than a league of friendship among the states, for each state retained nearly all its sovereign powers, and very little authority was handed over to the congress of delegates which was the official organ of the Confederation.

The Critical Period

It was under this makeshift arrangement that the thirteen states managed to make a formal treaty of peace with England in 1783 and to wrestle somewhat ineffectively with various other difficult problems during the next few years. These years formed a very critical period in American history. The states were growing jealous of each other, and some of them were already endeavoring by restrictive trade regulations to gain prosperity at the expense of their neighbors. In some cases, again, the boundaries between states had never been authoritatively fixed; rival claims were being pressed, and it looked as though some of the states would soon come to blows over such matters. As for the Congress of the Confederation, it had no power to compel a state to do anything; it had no revenues except such grants of money as the various states might make;

and it had no authority to regulate commerce in the common interest. It did not even possess power to make the states fulfill the terms of the treaty with England which it had made on their behalf in 1783.

The Need of a Stronger Union

Under these circumstances it soon became apparent to thoughtful men that the Confederation must be either strengthened or dissolved; that no useful purpose would be served by continuing it in impotence. To abandon it altogether was something hardly to be considered, for that would have opened wide the door to interstate quarrels and this, in turn, would have invited foreign intervention. The only alternative was to make the union a real one with a central authority strong enough to insure united action in all matters of common interest. To be efficient in this direction it was felt that the central government would require three powers not given to it by the Articles of Confederation: (1) the power to raise revenue and to borrow money without recourse to the states; (2) the power to regulate foreign and interstate commerce; (3) the exclusive power of making and enforcing treaties. It was well realized that the several states were likely to surrender any such powers very grudgingly, if at all; but in 1787 twelve of them were finally induced to send delegates to Philadelphia in order that the whole problem should be carefully considered.

The Constitutional Convention of 1787

Among the delegates who came to this convention were many men of great influence in their own communities. Washington, Madison and Randolph were on hand as representatives of Virginia. Jefferson could not be a delegate as he was at the time on a diplomatic mission to France. Pennsylvania sent Benjamin Franklin, James Wilson, John Dickinson, Robert Morris, Gouverneur Morris and others. New York looked askance at the whole proceeding but had among her three delegates an able representative in Alexander Hamilton. Other men of almost equal power and personality were there: Roger Sherman and Oliver Ellsworth from Connecticut; Elbridge Gerry and Rufus King from Massachusetts; William Paterson from New Jersey; and Luther Martin from Maryland. After some delay, due to the tardy arrival of delegates from several of the states, the convention organized, chose Washington as its presiding officer, and set to work on its great task.

Work of the Convention

For over three months during the discomforts of an unusually hot summer the convention met almost every week day. Its sessions were not open to the public and the delegates were enjoined to secrecy. All observed this rule faithfully and nothing reached the public ear concerning the deliberations until the whole work was finished. A formal record of the convention's proceedings was kept by the secretary; but this official performed his duty rather poorly, and our best account of what went on during the sessions has come down to us in the form of notes taken day by day for his own use by James Madison, who was the most regular attendant and the most active figure of the entire convention. A few other members of the convention made fragmentary notes or memoranda, so that posterity, by piecing everything together, has managed to get a fairly comprehensive and accurate account of the day-to-day proceedings.

The Randolph and Paterson Plans

It did not take the convention long to discover that widely divergent views concerning what ought to be done were held by different delegates. Some of them, including Hamilton and Madison, wanted a strong central government with plenty of coercive power lodged in its hands. Others, like Paterson and Martin, desired that the convention should proceed no further than to a slight strengthening of the powers given to the central government by the Articles of Confederation. Two outlines, known respectively as the Randolph and Paterson plans, were presented to the convention embodying these divergent views. The Randolph plan contemplated a reorganized union with a strong central government which should include legislative, executive and judicial departments. It proposed, moreover, that the central congress should be made up of representatives from the various states in proportion to their population, thereby setting aside the principle of equal state representation which had been recognized in the Articles of Confederation. The Paterson plan proposed no more than a revision of these Articles with a view chiefly to some enlargement in the powers of the Congress which should continue to give the states equality of representation despite their great differences in area and population.

The Basis of State Representation

Much of their time was spent by the members of the convention in discussing this fundamental question as to whether the central legislative authority of the union should be made up of representatives from the states in numbers proportioned to their population or whether each state should have the same quota of representatives. For a time it looked as if the work of the convention would come to naught through the failure of delegates to reach any agreement on this issue. The delegates from the larger states saw no good reason why Virginia, Pennsylvania and those states which would naturally furnish most of the common revenue should not have a controlling voice in the raising and spending of money. The delegates from Maryland, New Jersey and other small states were just as fully convinced that unless all were given equal representation the union would pass under the complete control of their more populous neighbors.

The Great Compromise

This difficulty was finally overcome, however, by the convention's acceptance of the Great Compromise. In brief, this compromise, which was brought before the convention by the delegates from Connecticut, provided for a Congress of two chambers, the upper chamber affording equal representation to all the states, the lower chamber representing the states according to their respective populations. It was further provided that all bills for raising and appropriating money should originate in the lower chamber and should not be subject to alteration or amendment in the upper house of Congress. Before the convention finished its work, however, this last provision was somewhat modified and the final draft of the new Constitution gave the lower house considerably less power in regard to financial matters than was contemplated by the terms of this compromise.

The Commerce Power

Having settled this crucial problem of representation the convention made better progress. But other difficult questions soon arose. One of these concerned the power which it was proposed to give Congress in the matter of customs taxes. The interests of the Northern and the Southern states seemed to diverge on this point, the former being willing to give Congress a large range of power, the latter desiring that its authority in the matter of taxing imports and exports should be limited. In the end it was agreed that Congress should be left free in its power to tax imports (except slaves) but that no tax should ever be laid on exports from any state.

Slavery

Then there were the difficult questions concerning slavery. In the first place there was opposition to the adoption of any arrangement which would make necessary for all time the continuance of the African slave traffic, and this opposition came not only from some of the Northern states but from Virginia as well. On the other hand the extreme Southern states, such as the Carolinas and Georgia, were rigid in their refusal to concede to Congress any power which would enable that body to prohibit at once the further importation of slaves. This conflict of interests was finally adjusted by withholding from

Congress the right to prohibit the importation of slaves during the first two decades after the Constitution went into force. In the meantime no import tax of more than ten dollars per slave was to be imposed.

The Three-Fifths Compromise

Another question connected with the institution of slavery likewise gave the convention some difficulty, although not so much as later writers on the subject seem to have imagined. It will be remembered that by the terms of the Great Compromise, it had been arranged to have representation in the lower house of Congress apportioned among the states according to their respective populations. But were slaves to be counted in determining a state's population? Delegates from the states of the North, where slaves were few, held that slaves should not be counted as a basis of representation; delegates from the states of the South, where slaves formed a very considerable part of the entire population, insisted that they should be counted. A somewhat illogical settlement of this point was made by the Three-Fifths Compromise. It was agreed that slaves should be counted in determining the quota of representatives which a state should have in Congress, but at three fifths of their numerical strength only. In other words, one hundred slaves were to be counted, for purposes of representation, as the equivalent of sixty free men. There was little logic, of course, in this compromise. If slaves were citizens they should have been counted at their full numerical value; if they were mere chattels, they should not have been counted at all. The terms of the Three-Fifths Compromise were arranged on the idea that they were neither the one thing nor the other. Nevertheless, the fact that the members of the convention were willing to accept this arrangement, illogical as it was, is a tribute to their sound political sense. They were not wedded to logic or theory in government. They realized that their first task was to put some sort of central government on its feet and to desire the end was to tolerate the means.

The Chief Executive

Various other matters made heavy demands upon the time and patience of the delegates. The proper position and authority of the executive head of the new federation was one of these. It was desired to provide for a president who would have dignity and powers commensurate with his position as the first citizen of a great nation; on the other hand it was just as strongly felt that the safety of a republican government required a due restriction of executive authority. The president was accordingly given great powers (*e.g.*, the appointing and veto powers), but effective provision was made to forestall any future abuse of his authority. To do all this required the working out of wholly new details of government. When it came to providing potential legislative checks upon a powerful executive there were no foreign precedents to follow. The convention had to break new ground. James Madison had drawn up for his own use a set of "Notes on Ancient and Modern Confederacies" which covered the whole historical range of European experiments in federal government from the Achæan League to the Helvetic Republic. But these notes were more useful in showing what to avoid than in pointing safe routes to be followed. We have had many successful experiments in federalism during the last hundred years — in Canada, Germany, Australia, South Africa, and elsewhere; but in 1787 the history of federal government was on the whole a chronicle of failures, partial or complete. It took courage to plan as boldly as the men of the Philadelphia convention planned; but the quality of courage was not lacking among the members of this body, some of whom had, eleven years before, put their signatures to the most daring document of their time.

Influence of Montesquieu

When one looks at the work of the constitutional convention in a broad way, there are two fundamental motives which appear to have guided the members. In the first place they agreed with the French philosopher, Montesquieu, that no particular frame of government is suited to all men in all ages and in all places. That form of government is best which best suits its environment. If the delegates were not, as a body, proficient in political theory they were thoroughly conversant with the New World's problems and with the political psychology of its people. Most of them had been in public life either as members of the Continental Congress, as governors of states, or as state officers. No one can read the records of the convention without realizing that it contained among its members many politicians of a very shrewd and practical type. They set out to draft a frame of government which would suit the genius of the American people, and this latter test was, for the most part, the only one that they applied. The constitutional history of the United States during the last hundred and twenty-five years is a sufficient testimony to their sagacity in this regard.

Attitude of Delegates towards the New Constitution

In the second place the convention was actuated by a desire to plan a scheme of government to which, in the words of Washington, " the wise and honest might repair," even though all its arrangements might not command the whole-hearted approval of any single delegate among its members. On great and small issues alike it was ready to compromise at all times, provided a safe and fair arrangement, duly regardful of every interest concerned, could be secured thereby. But it was not ready to adopt compromises for the sole purpose of drawing support to the new Constitution from the selfish and capricious elements in the national population. In other words, the members of the convention desired to frame a constitution that would gain acceptance at the hands of the people; but they also wanted to create a government that would endure. It is doubtful, therefore, whether the finished work of the convention commanded the unqualified approval of any one among the fifty-five who had a hand in making it. Only thirty-nine signed it; the other twenty-six had either left the convention before the new

Constitution was finished or declined to put their signatures to it at the convention's final session. Even among the thirty-nine who signed there were many serious doubters. Alexander Hamilton gave his signature gladly; but at the same time took occasion to remind the convention that no man's ideas were more remote from the new Constitution than his own. He realized that the new plan of government was likely to prove vastly superior to the old, and this seemed a sufficient reason for ranging himself with its supporters. Benjamin Franklin also had his misgivings; but after remarking that the experience of a long life had taught him to doubt the infallibility of his own opinions, he placed his name at the head of the Pennsylvania delegation. So it was with James Madison, who had done more than any other man to bring the work of the convention to a fruitful end. The final draft of the Constitution was not a mirror of his own political theories, but he was ready to shoulder his share of responsibility for it. There was a willingness to sink personal prejudices in a common effort to get what seemed to be the only scheme of central government on which there had been any approach to agreement. All those who signed the Constitution felt that it promised at least some improvement over the Articles of Confederation, but with several members of the convention that was the limit of their enthusiasm for it. To men of strong native convictions this action required both patriotism and courage, and in neither of these qualities was the constitutional convention found wanting.

II. THE CAMPAIGN FOR ITS ADOPTION

The Constitution before the States

When the convention completed its work on September 17, 1787, the real campaign for the establishment of the new government was still ahead: for the convention had no final powers; the new Constitution required the indorsement of at least nine states before it could go into force. So the document was sent to the Congress of the Confederation, which in turn transmitted copies of it without comment to the legislatures of the thirteen states in order that these might submit it for ratification. In none of the states was the Constitution submitted to popular vote, although several of the states had adopted their own state constitutions in that way. Instead, the people of each state were asked to choose delegates to a state convention, and to these conventions the Constitution was turned over for acceptance or rejection. Thereupon the whole country fairly seethed with warm discussion, the friends and foes of the new Constitution quickly ranging themselves into opposite camps. Letters poured into the newspapers; broadsides and pamphlets attacking the new scheme of government began to appear in profusion. It looked as though the Constitution stood little chance of acceptance unless some of the criticisms that were coming from all sides could be promptly and effectively answered.

Importance of New York

The pivotal point in the struggle was New York; for unless that state should accept the Constitution the new union would be split in twain. New York was not only one of the largest, most populous and most influential of the thirteen states, but geographically lay right athwart the country. Four states were to the north of her and eight to the south. No union could be solid without New York. It was in this state, rather ominously, that the most determined and best organized opposition to the new arrangements came forward, and it was here that regular newspapers afforded the largest opportunity for impressing the defects of the proposed Constitution on the public mind.

The Fault-Finders

It has been mentioned that the convention of 1787 met behind closed doors and that nothing was allowed to reach the public ear until its entire work was done. Naturally enough the new Constitution contained many surprises and its publication, as might have been expected, let loose an avalanche of criticism, mostly ill-tempered. Some critics complained that it gave the federal government too much power; others that it did not give enough. From all sides came the very serious and well-founded complaint that the Constitution contained no bill of rights; in other words that it afforded no securities for freedom of speech, for the freedom of the press, for trial by jury, and for the other so-termed natural rights of men and citizens. Clergymen throughout the land stigmatized the new Constitution as a sacrilegious document because it contained no mention of the Deity; others rebelled against the compromise with slavery; while many took the extreme ground that the convention had far exceeded its powers in framing a new Constitution, since it had been authorized only to suggest alterations in the old Articles of Confederation.

III. WHY THE FEDERALIST WAS WRITTEN

Hamilton's Plan

Under such circumstances it became necessary for the friends of the Constitution to get together, and especially to see that the critics of the convention did not have things all their own way in the newspapers. This they did under the leadership of Alexander Hamilton who mapped out for them a vigorous publicity campaign. Hamilton planned a series of newspaper letters which would take up the Constitution point by point, and would form, when completed, both an exposition of the whole document and a defence of its fundamental principles. This project he communicated to James Madison and John Jay with the request that they should help him to write the letters. Both agreed, and during the winter and spring of 1787–1788, eighty-five letters on the subject were printed, sometimes three or four a week, in the New York *Independent Journal*, the New York *Packet*, the New York *Daily Advertiser*, and the *Daily Patriotic Register*. Each letter dealt with some phase of the subject in logical order, explaining, defending and appealing to the public spirit of readers.

Hamilton's Services

Hamilton had been one of the younger members of the convention; he was now only thirty-one years of age. Educated at King's College (now Columbia University), he had served in the Revolutionary War as a member of Washington's staff and finished the campaign with the rank of colonel. During the meetings of the constitutional convention he was forced by the pressure of his private business affairs to be absent a great deal, so that his influence on the course of the deliberations was not large. But this was more than offset by the torrent of zeal and energy which he poured into the subsequent campaign. He had a mind of rare analytical power, and he could write clear, forceful English. Both of these gifts he used to the utmost in the cause which he had so much at heart during the struggles of 1787–1788. The lion's share of the newspaper propaganda came to him and he carried it all with signal success.

James Madison

For his friend and colleague, James Madison, the New York statesman had an unbounded personal admiration. Hamilton had seen some of Madison's work in the convention and had been deeply impressed. So, when things seemed to be moving badly in New York, the Virginian's abilities were called upon, and Madison's letters contributed greatly to the effectiveness of The Federalist. Madison also was a young man, but his knowledge of history was unrivaled in America. For many years he had been a close student of public affairs, both past and present; with the exception of Benjamin Franklin he was the most erudite member of the convention. His historical knowledge greatly impressed the other members and he probably had more influence in molding the Constitution than any other man. Madison knew the document as no one else knew it; hence it is that his contributions to The Federalist, while not showing those flashes of brilliancy which so often mark the writings of Hamilton, display a mastery of details and great skill in harmonizing them into a solid system. For his work both in making and defending the Constitution the Republic owes him all the homage that posterity can render.

John Jay

The third member of the Federalist trio, John Jay, was an able New Yorker who had not been a member of the constitutional convention but who possessed (what both Hamilton and Madison lacked) some acquaintance with diplomatic and foreign affairs. Jay's part in the writing of The Federalist was not large; his letters dealt only with such matters as the foreign dangers of disunion and the treaty-making powers of the new federal government. In handling these topics his experience as a diplomat gave him proficiency.

Authorship of the Letters

All the letters bore the common signature "Publius" and the exact authorship of several of them has been the theme of a controversy into the merits of which it is scarcely worth while to go; but it is beyond question that Hamilton carried the brunt of the whole undertaking. He not only planned the series but wrote at least fifty of the eighty-five letters. Of the remainder, twenty or more were probably written by James Madison, and five by John Jay. The exact authorship of the other letters is not absolutely certain; but some were written by Hamilton and Madison together, and it is practically certain that no one outside the above-named trio had a share in writing any of them.

Hamilton's Influence

This newspaper campaign aided greatly in securing support for the Constitution not only in New York, where support was most urgently needed, but in other states as well. It was not until July 20, 1788, that New York indorsed the new scheme of government by a narrow majority of three votes in the state convention. Had it not been for Hamilton's literary enterprise there is every reason to believe, therefore, that New York would have declined to enter the new union and would thereby have dealt the entire scheme a rude setback. Too much credit cannot accordingly be given to him and to his associates for the vigorous way in which they threw their energies into the fight and by their frank appeals to the sober-minded element of New York won the most difficult battle of the whole campaign for ratification.

IV. THE FEDERALIST AS A TREATISE ON GOVERNMENT

The Letters Collected

Even before all the letters had appeared in the newspapers they were collected and published in book form under the title of *The Federalist: A Collection of Essays written in favor of the New Constitution* (New York, 1788). Since that time at least thirty editions of the work have appeared, several of them being in foreign languages. Although the letters were written hastily and as campaign polemics, they were the handiwork of men who were brimful of their subject and who knew, better than any others of their time, just what they were writing about. It probably never entered the mind of Hamilton that he was planning and writing a treatise on the science of federal government which would at once take rank as the best work on that subject in any language and which would hold its place as such a whole century after his day. Yet that is what The Federalist became and continues to be. It was the first notable survey of the history of federalism and the first systematic review of the principles of federal government. As such it acquired at the outset a high place in the literature of political science.

Importance of The Federalist

But The Federalist is more than a general treatise on federal government. It is an exposition and defence of that scheme of political organization which the thirteen states adopted in the later years of the eighteenth century. It is a contemporary exposition, struck off at white heat by the artisans whose handiwork the Constitution was, and as such it has qualities not given to most commentaries on American government. For keenness of analysis, cogency in the statement of arguments, adroitness in reply to critics, and brilliancy of literary style, The Federalist has stood unrivaled in the field of political literature for one hundred and twenty-five years. This position, almost unique among books of American authorship, it seems likely to hold for many years to come, since the circumstances under which The Federalist was written can hardly ever arise again in any land.

Its Value Today

The long period intervening since the Constitution went into force in 1788 has brought many important changes in the structure and functions of American government. Seventeen amendments have been added during this time, some of them of great significance, but none of them discussed in The Federalist. Changes of great importance have also been made by judicial interpretation until, in their actual application, some of the Constitution's original provisions cover a far wider range than any one could have foreseen in 1788. The Federalist is not, therefore, a reliable guide for those who seek to master the Constitution in its present-day application to the problems of the nation. No single book can furnish such a guide. Not only the provisions of the Constitution itself, but the federal statutes, the decisions of the federal courts, and that host of political customs and usages which have grown up during the last hundred years or more must be reckoned with by students of constitutional law. But as an explanation of what the Constitution contained at the time of its adoption, and of what its various provisions meant to those who placed them in the document, there is nothing that equals or even approaches The Federalist in usefulness.

Its Comprehensiveness

The letters which constitute The Federalist were written, as has been pointed out, in accordance with a plan. Hamilton seems to have bestowed a great deal of care in the preparation of this plan, for it covers the ground fully and leaves no important feature of the Constitution out of its survey. Each letter was intended to form a short but forceful essay on some topic within the scope of this plan, — each complete in itself yet forming an essential part of a sustained argument. To carry through such an undertaking successfully was no easy task, and when it is remembered that both Hamilton and Madison were otherwise very busy during the campaign for the adoption of the Constitution in New York and Virginia, respectively, the high standard of excellence attained by those Federalist letters deserves all the admiration that students of government have bestowed. The appeal of the writers was made to the fair-minded elements of the electorate, to those who were " unbiased by considerations not connected with the public good." Consequently The Federalist discussions assumed a plane high above that taken by the swarm of contemporary pamphlets whose writers appealed for the most part to petty prejudices and personal animosities. From the logic, style and temper of their respective arguments it was easy enough for the unprejudiced citizen to judge whether the supporters or opponents of the new Constitution had the public interest on their side, and the various state conventions in their final decisions merely recorded the convictions of the people whom they represented. With the lapse of a century the carping pamphlets and pamphleteers have been forgotten; the letters of The Federalist, on the other hand, have maintained their place as the most authoritative exposition of those principles and motives which guided the framers of the American Constitution in the performance of their monumental task.

V. BIBLIOGRAPHICAL NOTE

THERE have been many editions of *The Federalist;* but those most useful to the average student are Paul Leicester Ford, *The Federalist* (New York, 1898), and Henry Cabot Lodge, *The Federalist* (New York, 1900). The complete proceedings of the constitutional convention are in Max Farrand's *Records of the Federal Convention* (3 vols., New Haven, 1911); general narratives of the work of the convention may be found in the same writer's later volume on *The Framing of the Constitution of the United States* (New Haven, 1913), in George Bancroft's *History of the Formation of the Constitution* (2 vols., New York, 1883), especially II.; and in John Fiske's *Critical Period of American History* (Boston, 1902), ch. vi. Most of the important pamphlets issued by opponents of the Constitution are reprinted in Paul Leicester Ford's *Pamphlets on the Constitution* (Brooklyn, 1888). Further information concerning the public services of *The Federalist's* writers may be had in Henry Cabot Lodge's *Life of Alexander Hamilton* (Boston, 1882); in S. H. Gay's *James Madison* (Boston, 1884); and in George Pellew's *John Jay* (Boston, 1890). All three biographies are in the American Statesmen Series.

SELECTIONS FROM THE FEDERALIST

I

THE DANGERS OF DISUNION

(*a*) DANGERS FROM ABROAD

Concerning Dangers from Foreign Force and Influence [1]

When the people of America reflect that they are now called upon to decide a question, which, in its consequences, must prove one of the most important that ever engaged their attention, the propriety of their taking a very comprehensive, as well as a very serious, view of it will be evident.

Nothing is more certain than the indispensable necessity of government; and it is equally undeniable that whenever and however it is instituted, the people must cede to it some of their natural rights, in order to vest it with requisite powers. It is well worthy of consideration, therefore, whether it would conduce more to the interest of the people of America that they should, to all general purposes, be one nation, under one federal government, or that they should divide themselves into separate confederacies, and give to the head of each the same kind of powers which they are advised to place in one national government.

It has until lately been a received and uncontradicted opinion, that the prosperity of the people of America depended on their continuing firmly united; and the wishes, prayers, and efforts of our best and wisest citizens have been constantly directed

[1] No. II. Jay. Independent Journal, October 31, 1787.

to that object. But politicians now appear, who insist that this opinion is erroneous, and that instead of looking for safety and happiness in union, we ought to seek it in a division of the states into distinct confederacies or sovereignties. However extraordinary this new doctrine may appear, it nevertheless has its advocates; and certain characters who were much opposed to it formerly, are at present of the number. Whatever may be the arguments or inducements which have wrought this change in the sentiments and declarations of these gentlemen, it certainly would not be wise in the people at large to adopt these new political tenets, without being fully convinced that they are founded on truth and sound policy.

It has often given me pleasure to observe, that independent America was not composed of detached and distant territories, but that one connected, fertile, wide-spreading country was the portion of our western sons of liberty. Providence has in a particular manner blessed it with a variety of soils and productions, and watered it with innumerable streams, for the delight and accommodation of its inhabitants. A succession of navigable waters forms a kind of chain round its borders, as if to bind it together; while the most noble rivers in the world, running at convenient distances, present them with highways for the easy communication of friendly aids, and the mutual transportation and exchange of their various commodities.

With equal pleasure I have as often taken notice that Providence has been pleased to give this one connected country to one united people, a people descended from the same ancestors, speaking the same language, professing the same religion, attached to the same principles of government, very similar in their manners and customs, and who, by their joint counsels, arms and efforts, fighting side by side throughout a long and bloody war, have nobly established their general liberty and independence.

This country and this people seem to have been made for each other; and it appears as if it was the design of Providence, that an inheritance so proper and convenient for a band of brethren, united to each other by the strongest ties, should never be split into a number of unsocial, jealous, and alien sovereignties.

Similar sentiments have hitherto prevailed among all orders and denominations of men among us. To all general purposes, we have uniformly been one people — each individual citizen everywhere enjoying the same national rights, privileges, and protection. As a nation we have made peace and war; as a nation we have vanquished our common enemies; as a nation we have formed alliances and made treaties, and entered into various compacts and conventions with foreign states.

A strong sense of the value and blessings of union induced the people, at a very early period, to institute a federal government to preserve and perpetuate it. They formed it almost as soon as they had a political existence; nay, at a time when their habitations were in flames, when many of their citizens were bleeding, and when the progress of hostility and desolation left little room for those calm and mature inquiries and reflections, which must ever precede the formation of a wise and well-balanced government for a free people. It is not to be wondered at that a government instituted in times so inauspicious, should on experiment be found greatly deficient, and inadequate to the purpose it was intended to answer.

This intelligent people perceived and regretted these defects. Still continuing no less attached to union than enamored of liberty, they observed the danger which immediately threatened the former and more remotely the latter; and being persuaded that ample security for both could only be found in a national government more wisely framed, they, as with one voice, convened the late Convention at Philadelphia, to take that important subject under consideration.

This Convention, composed of men who possessed the confidence of the people, and many of whom had become highly distinguished by their patriotism, virtue and wisdom, in times which tried the minds and hearts of men, undertook the arduous task. In the mild season of peace, with minds unoccupied by other subjects, they passed many months in cool, uninterrupted, and daily consultations; and finally, without having been awed by power, or influenced by any passions, except love for their country, they presented and recommended to the people the plan produced by their joint and very unanimous councils.

Admit, for so is the fact, that this plan is only *recommended*, not imposed, yet let it be remembered that it is neither recommended to *blind* approbation, nor to *blind* reprobation, but to that sedate and candid consideration which the magnitude and importance of the subject demand, and which it certainly ought to receive. But, as has been already remarked, it is more to be wished than expected that it may be so considered and examined. Experience on a former occasion teaches us not to be too sanguine in such hopes. It is not yet forgotten that well-grounded apprehensions of imminent danger induced the people of America to form the memorable Congress of 1774. That body recommended certain measures to their constituents, and the event proved their wisdom; yet it is fresh in our memories how soon the press began to teem with pamphlets and weekly papers against those very measures. Not only many of the officers of government, who obeyed the dictates of personal interest, but others, from a mistaken estimate of consequences, from the undue influence of ancient attachments, or whose ambition aimed at objects which did not correspond with the public good, were indefatigable in their endeavors to persuade the people to reject the advice of that patriotic Congress. Many, indeed, were deceived and deluded, but the great majority of the people reasoned and decided judiciously; and happy they are in reflecting that they did so.

They considered that the Congress was composed of many wise and experienced men. That, being convened from different parts of the country, they brought with them and communicated to each other a variety of useful information. That, in the course of the time they passed together in inquiring into and discussing the true interests of their country, they must have acquired very accurate knowledge on that head. That they were individually interested in the public liberty and prosperity, and therefore that it was not less their inclination than their duty to recommend only such measures as, after the most mature deliberation, they really thought prudent and advisable.

These and similar considerations then induced the people to rely greatly on the judgment and integrity of the Congress; and they took their advice, notwithstanding the various arts and endeavors used to deter and dissuade them from it. But if the people at large had reason to confide in the men of that Congress, few of whom had then been fully tried or generally known, still greater reason have they now to respect the judgment and advice of the Convention, for it is well known that some of the most distinguished members of that Congress, who have been since tried and justly approved for patriotism and abilities, and who have grown old in acquiring political information, were also members of this Convention, and carried into it their accumulated knowledge and experience.

It is worthy of remark that not only the first, but every succeeding Congress, as well as the late Convention, have invariably joined with the people in thinking that the prosperity of America depended on its Union. To preserve and perpetuate it was the great object of the people in forming that Convention, and it is also the great object of the plan which the Convention has advised them to adopt. With what propriety, therefore, or for what good purposes, are attempts at this particular period made by some men to depreciate the importance of the Union? Or why is it suggested that three or four confederacies would be better than one? I am persuaded in my own mind that the people have always thought right on this subject, and that their universal and uniform attachment to the cause of the Union rests on great and weighty reasons, which I shall endeavor to develop and explain in some ensuing papers. They who promote the idea of substituting a number of distinct confederacies in the room of the plan of the Convention, seem clearly to foresee that the rejection of it would put the continuance of the Union in the utmost jeopardy. That certainly would be the case, and I sincerely wish that it may be as clearly foreseen by every good citizen, that whenever the dissolution of the Union arrives, America will have reason to exclaim, in the words of the poet, "FAREWELL! A LONG FAREWELL, TO ALL MY GREATNESS!"

PUBLIUS.

THE SAME SUBJECT CONTINUED[1]

It is not a new observation that the people of any country (if, like the Americans, intelligent and well-informed) seldom adopt and steadily persevere for many years in an erroneous opinion respecting their interests. That consideration naturally tends to create great respect for the high opinion which the people of America have so long and uniformly entertained of the importance of their continuing firmly united under one federal government, vested with sufficient powers for all general and national purposes.

The more attentively I consider and investigate the reasons which appear to have given birth to this opinion, the more I become convinced that they are cogent and conclusive.

Among the many objects to which a wise and free people find it necessary to direct their attention, that of providing for their *safety* seems to be the first. The *safety* of the people doubtless has relation to a great variety of circumstances and considerations, and consequently affords great latitude to those who wish to define it precisely and comprehensively.

At present I mean only to consider it as it respects security for the preservation of peace and tranquillity, as well against dangers from *foreign arms and influence* as from dangers of the *like kind* arising from domestic causes. As the former of these comes first in order, it is proper it should be the first discussed. Let us therefore proceed to examine whether the people are not right in their opinion that a cordial union, under an efficient national government, affords them the best security that can be devised against *hostilities* from abroad.

The number of wars which have happened or will happen in the world will always be found to be in proportion to the number

[1] No. III. Jay. Independent Journal, November 3, 1787.

and weight of the causes, whether *real* or *pretended*, which *provoke* or *invite* them. If this remark be just, it becomes useful to inquire whether so many *just* causes of war are likely to be given by *united* America as by *disunited* America; for if it should turn out that united America will probably give the fewest, then it will follow that in this respect the union tends most to preserve the people in a state of peace with other nations.

The *just* causes of war, for the most part, arise either from violations of treaties or from direct violence. America has already formed treaties with no less than six foreign nations, and all of them, except Prussia, are maritime, and therefore able to annoy and injure us. She has also extensive commerce with Portugal, Spain, and Britain, and, with respect to the two latter, has, in addition, the circumstance of neighborhood to attend to.

It is of high importance to the peace of America that she observe the laws of nations towards all these powers, and to me it appears evident that this will be more perfectly and punctually done by one national government than it could be either by thirteen separate states or by three or four distinct confederacies. For this opinion various reasons may be assigned. When once an efficient national government is established, the best men in the country will not only consent to serve, but also will generally be appointed to manage it; for, although town or country, or other contracted influence, may place men in state assemblies, or senates, or courts of justice, or executive departments, yet more general and extensive reputation for talents and other qualifications will be necessary to recommend men to offices under the national government, especially as it will have the widest field for choice, and never experience that want of proper persons which is not uncommon in some of the states. Hence, it will result that the administration, the political counsels, and the judicial decisions of the national government will be more wise, systematical, and judicious than those of individual states, and consequently more satisfactory with respect to other nations, as well as more *safe* with respect to us.

Under the national government, treaties and articles of treaties, as well as the laws of nations, will always be expounded in one sense and executed in the same manner, whereas adjudications on the same points and questions, in thirteen states, or in three or four confederacies, will not always accord or be consistent; and that, as well from the variety of independent courts and judges appointed by different and independent governments, as from the different local laws and interests which may affect and influence them. The wisdom of the Convention, in committing such questions to the jurisdiction and judgment of courts appointed by and responsible only to one national government, cannot be too much commended.

The prospect of present loss or advantage may often tempt the governing party in one or two states to swerve from good faith and justice; but those temptations, not reaching the other states, and consequently having little or no influence on the national government, the temptations will be fruitless, and good faith and justice be preserved. The case of the treaty of peace with Britain adds great weight to this reasoning.

If even the governing party in a state should be disposed to resist such temptations, yet, as such temptations may, and commonly do, result from circumstances peculiar to the state, and may affect a great number of the inhabitants, the governing party may not always be able, if willing, to prevent the injustice meditated, or to punish the aggressors. But the national government, not being affected by those local circumstances, will neither be induced to commit the wrong themselves, nor want power or inclination to prevent or punish its commission by others.

So far, therefore, as either designed or accidental violations of treaties and of the laws of nations afford *just* causes of war, they are less to be apprehended under one general government than under several lesser ones, and in that respect the former most favors the *safety* of the people.

As to those just causes of war which proceed from direct and unlawful violence, it appears equally clear to me that one good national government affords vastly more security against dangers of that sort than can be derived from any other quarter.

Such violences are more frequently occasioned by the passions and interests of a part than of the whole, of one or two states than of the Union. Not a single Indian war has yet been produced by aggressions of the present federal government, feeble as it is; but there are several instances of Indian hostilities having been provoked by the improper conduct of individual states, which, either unable or unwilling to restrain or punish offenses, have given occasion to the slaughter of many innocent inhabitants.

The neighborhood of Spanish and British territories, bordering on some states and not on others, naturally confines the causes of quarrel more immediately to the borderers. The bordering states, if any, will be those who, under the impulse of sudden irritation, and a quick sense of apparent interest or injury, will be most likely, by direct violence, to excite war with those nations; and nothing can so effectually obviate that danger as a national government, whose wisdom and prudence will not be diminished by the passions which actuate the parties immediately interested.

But not only fewer just causes of war will be given by the national government, but it will also be more in their power to accommodate and settle them amicably. They will be more temperate and cool, and in that respect, as well as in others, will be more in capacity to act with circumspection than the offending state. The pride of states, as well as of men, naturally disposes them to justify all their actions, and opposes their acknowledging, correcting, or repairing their errors and offenses. The national government, in such cases, will not be affected by this pride, but will proceed with moderation and candor to consider and decide on the means most proper to extricate them from the difficulties which threaten them.

Besides, it is well known that acknowledgments, explanations, and compensations are often accepted as satisfactory from a strong united nation, which would be rejected as unsatisfactory if offered by a state or confederacy of little consideration or power.

In the year 1685, the state of Genoa having offended Louis XIV, endeavored to appease him. He demanded that they should send their *Doge*, or chief magistrate, accompanied by four of their senators, to *France*, to ask his pardon and receive his terms. They were obliged to submit to it for the sake of peace. Would he on any occasion either have demanded or have received the like humiliation from Spain, or Britain, or any other *powerful* nation?

PUBLIUS.

THE SAME SUBJECT CONTINUED [1]

My last paper assigned several reasons why the safety of the people would be best secured by union against the danger it may be exposed to by *just* causes of war given to other nations; and those reasons show that such causes would not only be more rarely given, but would also be more easily accommodated, by a national government than either by the state governments or the proposed confederacies.

But the safety of the people of America against dangers from *foreign* force depends not only on their forbearing to give *just* causes of war to other nations, but also on their placing and continuing themselves in such a situation as not to *invite* hostility or insult; for it need not be observed that there are *pretended* as well as just causes of war.

It is too true, however disgraceful it may be to human nature, that nations in general will make war whenever they have a prospect of getting anything by it; nay, that absolute monarchs will often make war when their nations are to get nothing by it, but for purposes and objects merely personal, such as a thirst for military glory, revenge for personal affronts, ambition, or private compacts to aggrandize or support their particular families or partisans. These and a variety of motives, which affect only the mind of the sovereign, often lead him to engage in wars not sanctified by justice or the voice and interests of his people.

[1] No. IV. Jay. Independent Journal, November 7, 1787.

But, independent of these inducements to war, which are most prevalent in absolute monarchies, but which well deserve our attention, there are others which affect nations as often as kings; and some of them will on examination be found to grow out of our relative situation and circumstances.

With France and with Britain we are rivals in the fisheries, and can supply their markets cheaper than they can themselves, notwithstanding any efforts to prevent it by bounties on their own or duties on foreign fish.

With them and most other European nations we are rivals in navigation and the carrying trade; and we shall deceive ourselves, if we suppose that any of them will rejoice to see it flourish; for, as our carrying trade cannot increase without in some degree diminishing theirs, it is more their interest, and will be more their policy, to restrain than to promote it.

In the trade to China and India, we interfere with more than one nation, inasmuch as it enables us to partake in advantages which they had in a manner monopolized, and as we thereby supply ourselves with commodities which we used to purchase from them.

The extension of our own commerce in our own vessels cannot give pleasure to any nations who possess territories on or near this continent, because the cheapness and excellence of our productions, added to the circumstance of vicinity, and the enterprise and address of our merchants and navigators, will give us a greater share in the advantages which those territories afford, than consists with the wishes or policy of their respective sovereigns.

Spain thinks it convenient to shut the Mississippi against us on the one side, and Britain excludes us from the St. Lawrence on the other; nor will either of them permit the other waters which are between them and us to become the means of mutual intercourse and traffic.

From these and such like considerations, which might, if consistent with prudence, be more amplified and detailed, it is easy to see that jealousies and uneasinesses may gradually slide into the minds and cabinets of other nations, and that we are not to expect that they should regard our advancement in union, in power and consequence by land and by sea, with an eye of indifference and composure.

The people of America are aware that inducements to war may arise out of these circumstances, as well as from others not so obvious at present, and that whenever such inducements may find fit time and opportunity for operation, pretenses to color and justify them will not be wanting. Wisely, therefore, do they consider union and a good national government as necessary to put and keep them in *such a situation* as, instead of *inviting* war, will tend to repress and discourage it. That situation consists in the best possible state of defense, and necessarily depends on the government, the arms, and the resources of the country.

As the safety of the whole is the interest of the whole, and cannot be provided for without government, either one or more or many, let us inquire whether one good government is not, relative to the object in question, more competent than any other given number whatever.

One government can collect and avail itself of the talents and experience of the ablest men, in whatever part of the Union they may be found. It can move on uniform principles of policy. It can harmonize, assimilate, and protect the several parts and members, and extend the benefit of its foresight and precautions to each. In the formation of treaties, it will regard the interest of the whole, and the particular interests of the parts as connected with that of the whole. It can apply the resources and power of the whole to the defense of any particular part, and that more easily and expeditiously than state governments or separate confederacies can possibly do, for want of concert and unity of system. It can place the militia under one plan of discipline, and, by putting their officers in a proper line of subordination to the chief magistrate, will in a manner consolidate them into one corps, and thereby render them more efficient than if divided into thirteen or into three or four distinct independent bodies.

What would the militia of Britain be if the English militia obeyed the government of England, if the Scotch militia obeyed the government of Scotland, and if the Welsh militia obeyed the government of Wales? Suppose an invasion: would those three governments (if they agreed at all) be able, with all their respective forces, to operate against the enemy so effectually as the single government of Great Britain would?

We have heard much of the fleets of Britain, and the time may come, if we are wise, when the fleets of America may engage attention. But if one national government had not so regulated the navigation of Britain as to make it a nursery for seamen, if one national government had not called forth all the national means and materials for forming fleets, their prowess and their thunder would never have been celebrated. Let England have its navigation and fleet — let Scotland have its navigation and fleet — let Wales have its navigation and fleet — let Ireland have its navigation and fleet — let those four of the constituent parts of the British empire be under four independent governments, and it is easy to perceive how soon they would each dwindle into comparative insignificance.

Apply these facts to our own case. Leave America divided into thirteen or, if you please, into three or four independent governments, — what armies could they raise and pay, what fleets could they ever hope to have? If one was attacked, would the others fly to its succor, and spend their blood and money in its defense? Would there be no danger of their being flattered into neutrality by specious promises, or seduced by a too great fondness for peace to decline hazarding their tranquillity and present safety for the sake of neighbors, of whom perhaps they have been jealous, and whose importance they are content to see diminished? Although such conduct would not be wise, it would, nevertheless, be natural. The history of the states of Greece, and of other countries, abounds with such instances, and it is not improbable that what has so often happened would, under similar circumstances, happen again.

But admit that they might be willing to help the invaded

state or confederacy. How, and when, and in what proportion shall aids of men and money be afforded? Who shall command the allied armies, and from which of them shall he receive his orders? Who shall settle the terms of peace, and in case of disputes what umpire shall decide between them and compel acquiescence? Various difficulties and inconveniences would be inseparable from such a situation; whereas one government, watching over the general and common interests, and combining and directing the powers and resources of the whole, would be free from all these embarrassments, and conduce far more to the safety of the people.

But whatever may be our situation, whether firmly united under one national government, or split into a number of confederacies, certain it is that foreign nations will know and view it exactly as it is; and they will act towards us accordingly. If they see that our national government is efficient and well administered, our trade prudently regulated, our militia properly organized and disciplined, our resources and finances discreetly managed, our credit reëstablished, our people free, contented, and united, they will be much more disposed to cultivate our friendship than provoke our resentment. If, on the other hand, they find us either destitute of an effectual government (each state doing right or wrong, as to its rulers may seem convenient), or split into three or four independent and probably discordant republics or confederacies, one inclining to Britain, another to France, and a third to Spain, and perhaps played off against each other by the three, what a poor, pitiful figure will America make in their eyes! How liable would she become not only to their contempt, but to their outrage; and how soon would dear-bought experience proclaim that when a people or family so divide, it never fails to be against themselves.

PUBLIUS.

THE SAME SUBJECT CONTINUED [1]

Queen Anne, in her letter of the 1st July, 1706, to the Scotch Parliament, makes some observations on the importance of the *union* then forming between England and Scotland, which merit our attention. I shall present the public with one or two extracts from it: "An entire and perfect union will be the solid foundation of lasting peace: it will secure your religion, liberty, and property, remove the animosities amongst yourselves, and the jealousies and differences betwixt our two kingdoms. It must increase your strength, riches, and trade; and by this union the whole island, being joined in affection and free from all apprehensions of different interest, will be *enabled to resist all its enemies*." "We most earnestly recommend to you calmness and unanimity in this great and weighty affair, that the union may be brought to a happy conclusion, being the only *effectual* way to secure our present and future happiness; and disappoint the designs of our and your enemies, who will doubtless, on this occasion, *use their utmost endeavours to prevent or delay this union*."

It was remarked in the preceding paper, that weakness and divisions at home would invite dangers from abroad; and that nothing would tend more to secure us from them than union, strength, and good government within ourselves. This subject is copious and cannot easily be exhausted.

The history of Great Britain is the one with which we are in general the best acquainted, and gives us many useful lessons. We may profit by their experience without paying the price which it cost them. Although it seems obvious to common sense that the people of such an island should be but one nation, yet we find that they were for ages divided into three, and those three were almost constantly embroiled in quarrels and wars with one another. Notwithstanding their true interest with respect to the continental nations was really the same, yet by the arts and policy and practices of those nations, their

[1] No. V. Jay. Independent Journal, November 10, 1787.

mutual jealousies were perpetually kept inflamed, and for a long series of years they were far more inconvenient and troublesome than they were useful and assisting to each other.

Should the people of America divide themselves into three or four nations, would not the same thing happen? Would not similar jealousies arise, and be in like manner cherished? Instead of their being "joined in affection and free from all apprehension of different interests," envy and jealousy would soon extinguish confidence and affection, and the partial interests of each confederacy, instead of the general interests of all America, would be the only objects of their policy and pursuits. Hence, like most other *bordering* nations, they would always be either involved in disputes and war, or live in the constant apprehension of them.

The most sanguine advocates for three or four confederacies cannot reasonably suppose that they would long remain exactly on an equal footing in point of strength, even if it was possible to form them so at first; but, admitting that to be practicable, yet what human contrivance can secure the continuance of such equality? Independent of those local circumstances which tend to beget and increase power in one part and to impede its progress in another, we must advert to the effects of that superior policy and good management which would probably distinguish the government of one above the rest, and by which their relative equality in strength and consideration would be destroyed. For it cannot be presumed that the same degree of sound policy, prudence, and foresight would uniformly be observed by each of these confederacies for a long succession of years.

Whenever, and from whatever causes, it might happen, and happen it would, that any one of these nations or confederacies should rise on the scale of political importance much above the degree of her neighbors, that moment would those neighbors behold her with envy and with fear. Both those passions would lead them to countenance, if not to promote, whatever might promise to diminish her importance, and would also restrain them from measures calculated to advance or even to secure her prosperity. Much time would not be necessary to enable her to discern these unfriendly dispositions. She would soon begin, not only to lose confidence in her neighbors, but also to feel a disposition equally unfavorable to them. Distrust naturally creates distrust, and by nothing is good will and kind conduct more speedily changed than by invidious jealousies and uncandid imputations, whether expressed or implied.

The North is generally the region of strength, and many local circumstances render it probable that the most northern of the proposed confederacies would, at a period not very distant, be unquestionably more formidable than any of the others. No sooner would this become evident than the *Northern Hive* would excite the same ideas and sensations in the more southern parts of America which it formerly did in the southern parts of Europe. Nor does it appear to be a rash conjecture that its young swarms might often be tempted to gather honey in the more blooming fields and milder air of their luxurious and more delicate neighbors.

They who well consider the history of similar divisions and confederacies will find abundant reason to apprehend that those in contemplation would in no other sense be neighbors than as they would be borderers; that they would neither love nor trust one another, but on the contrary would be a prey to discord, jealousy, and mutual injuries; in short, that they would place us exactly in the situation in which some nations doubtless wish to see us, viz., *formidable only to each other.*

From these considerations it appears that those persons are greatly mistaken who suppose that alliances offensive and defensive might be formed between these confederacies, and would produce that combination and union of wills, of arms, and of resources which would be necessary to put and keep them in a formidable state of defense against foreign enemies.

When did the independent states, into which Britain and Spain were formerly divided, combine in such alliances, or unite their forces against a foreign enemy? The proposed confederacies will be *distinct nations.* Each of them would have its commerce with foreigners to regulate by distinct treaties; and as their productions and commodities are different and proper for different markets, so would those treaties be essentially different. Different commercial concerns must create different interests, and of course different degrees of political attachment to and connection with different foreign nations. Hence it might and probably would happen that the foreign nation with whom the *Southern* confederacy might be at war would be the one with whom the *Northern* confederacy would be the most desirous of preserving peace and friendship. An alliance so contrary to their immediate interest would not therefore be easy to form, nor, if formed, would it be observed and fulfilled with perfect good faith.

Nay, it is far more probable that in America, as in Europe, neighboring nations, acting under the impulse of opposite interests and unfriendly passions, would frequently be found taking different sides. Considering our distance from Europe, it would be more natural for these confederacies to apprehend danger from one another than from distant nations, and therefore that each of them should be more desirous to guard against the others by the aid of foreign alliances, than to guard against foreign dangers by alliances between themselves. And here let us not forget how much more easy it is to receive foreign fleets into our ports, and foreign armies into our country, than it is to persuade or compel them to depart. How many conquests did the Romans and others make in the character of allies, and what innovations did they under the same character introduce into the governments of those whom they pretended to protect?

Let candid men judge, then, whether the division of America into any given number of independent sovereignties would tend to secure us against the hostilities and improper interference of foreign nations.

PUBLIUS.

(*b*) DANGERS AT HOME

CONCERNING DANGERS FROM WAR BETWEEN THE STATES[1]

The three last numbers of this paper have been dedicated to an enumeration of the dangers to which we should be exposed, in a state of disunion, from the arms and arts of foreign nations. I shall now proceed to delineate dangers of a different and, perhaps, still more alarming kind,— those which will in all probability flow from dissensions between the states themselves, and from domestic factions and convulsions. These have been already in some instances slightly anticipated; but they deserve a more particular and more full investigation.

A man must be far gone in Utopian speculations who can seriously doubt that, if these states should either be wholly disunited, or only united in partial confederacies, the sub-divisions into which they might be thrown would have frequent and violent contests with each other. To presume a want of motives for such contests as an argument against their existence, would be to forget that men are ambitious, vindictive, and rapacious. To look for a continuation of harmony between a number of independent, unconnected sovereignties situated in the same neighborhood, would be to disregard the uniform course of human events and to set at defiance the accumulated experience of ages.

The causes of hostility among nations are innumerable. There are some which have a general and almost constant operation upon the collective bodies of society. Of this description are the love of power or the desire of preëminence and dominion, the jealousy of power, or the desire of equality and safety. There are others which have a more circumscribed though an equally operative influence within their spheres. Such are the rivalships and competitions of commerce between commercial nations. And there are others, not less numerous than either

[1] No. VI. Hamilton. Independent Journal, November 14, 1787.

of the former, which take their origin entirely in private passions; in the attachments, enmities, interests, hopes, and fears of leading individuals in the communities of which they are members. Men of this class, whether the favorites of a king or of a people, have in too many instances abused the confidence they possessed; and assuming the pretext of some public motive, have not scrupled to sacrifice the national tranquillity to personal advantage or personal gratification.

The celebrated Pericles, in compliance with the resentments of a prostitute,[1] at the expense of much of the blood and treasure of his countrymen, attacked, vanquished, and destroyed the city of the *Samnians*. The same man, stimulated by private pique against the *Megarensians*,[2] another nation of Greece, or to avoid a prosecution with which he was threatened as an accomplice in a supposed theft of the statuary *Phidias*,[3] or to get rid of the accusations prepared to be brought against him for dissipating the funds of the state in the purchase of popularity,[4] or from a combination of all these causes, was the primitive author of that famous and fatal war, distinguished in the Grecian annals by the name of the *Peloponnesian* war; which, after various vicissitudes, intermissions, and renewals, terminated in the ruin of the Athenian commonwealth.

The ambitious cardinal, who was prime minister to Henry VIII, permitting his vanity to aspire to the triple crown,[5] entertained hopes of succeeding in the acquisition of that splendid prize by the influence of the Emperor Charles V. To secure the favor and interest of this enterprising and powerful monarch, he precipitated England into a war with France, contrary to the plainest dictates of policy, and at the hazard of the safety and independence, as well of the kingdom over which he presided by his counsels, as of Europe in general.

[1] Aspasia, vide Plutarch's *Life of Pericles*.

[2] *Ibid.*

[3] *Ibid.* Phidias was supposed to have stolen some public gold, with the connivance of Pericles, for the embellishment of the statue of Minerva.

[4] *Ibid.*

[5] Worn by the popes.

For if there ever was a sovereign who bid fair to realize the project of universal monarchy, it was the Emperor Charles V, of whose intrigues Wolsey was at once the instrument and the dupe.

The influence which the bigotry of one female,[1] the petulances of another,[2] and the cabals of a third,[3] had in the contemporary policy, ferments, and pacifications, of a considerable part of Europe, are topics that have been too often descanted upon not to be generally known.

To multiply examples of the agency of personal considerations in the production of great national events, either foreign or domestic, according to their direction, would be an unnecessary waste of time. Those who have but a superficial acquaintance with the sources from which they are to be drawn, will themselves recollect a variety of instances; and those who have a tolerable knowledge of human nature will not stand in need of such lights, to form their opinion either of the reality or extent of that agency. Perhaps, however, a reference, tending to illustrate the general principle, may with propriety be made to a case which has lately happened among ourselves. If Shays had not been a *desperate debtor*, it is much to be doubted whether Massachusetts would have been plunged into a civil war.

But notwithstanding the concurring testimony of experience in this particular, there are still to be found visionary or designing men who stand ready to advocate the paradox of perpetual peace between the states, though dismembered and alienated from each other. The genius of republics (say they) is pacific; the spirit of commerce has a tendency to soften the manners of men, and to extinguish those inflammable humors which have so often kindled into wars. Commercial republics, like ours, will never be disposed to waste themselves in ruinous contentions with each other. They will be governed by mutual

[1] Madame de Maintenon.
[2] Duchess of Marlborough.
[3] Madame de Pompadour.

interest, and will cultivate a spirit of mutual amity and concord.

Is it not (we may ask these projectors in politics) the true interest of all nations to cultivate the same benevolent and philosophic spirit? If this be their true interest, have they in fact pursued it? Has it not, on the contrary, invariably been found that momentary passions, and immediate interests, have a more active and imperious control over human conduct than general or remote considerations of policy, utility, or justice? Have republics in practice been less addicted to war than monarchies? Are not the former administered by *men* as well as the latter? Are there not aversions, predilections, rivalships, and desires of unjust acquisition, that affect nations as well as kings? Are not popular assemblies frequently subject to the impulses of rage, resentment, jealousy, avarice, and of other irregular and violent propensities? Is it not well known that their determinations are often governed by a few individuals in whom they place confidence, and are, of course, liable to be tinctured by the passions and views of those individuals? Has commerce hitherto done anything more than change the objects of war? Is not the love of wealth as domineering and enterprising a passion as that of power or glory? Have there not been as many wars founded upon commercial motives since that has become the prevailing system of nations, as were before occasioned by the cupidity of territory or dominion? Has not the spirit of commerce, in many instances, administered new incentives to the appetite, both for the one and for the other? Let experience, the least fallible guide of human opinions, be appealed to for an answer to these inquiries.

Sparta, Athens, Rome, and Carthage were all republics, two of them, Athens and Carthage, of the commercial kind. Yet were they as often engaged in wars, offensive and defensive, as the neighboring monarchies of the same time. Sparta was little better than a well-regulated camp; and Rome was never sated of carnage and conquest.

Carthage, though a commercial republic, was the aggressor in the very war that ended in her destruction. Hannibal had carried her arms into the heart of Italy, and to the gates of Rome, before Scipio, in turn, gave him an overthrow in the territories of Carthage, and made a conquest of the commonwealth.

Venice, in later times, figured more than once in wars of ambition, till, becoming an object of terror to the other Italian states, Pope Julius II found means to accomplish that formidable league,[1] which gave a deadly blow to the power and pride of that haughty republic.

The provinces of Holland, till they were overwhelmed in debts and taxes, took a leading and conspicuous part in the wars of Europe. They had furious contests with England for the dominion of the sea, and were among the most persevering and most implacable of the opponents of Louis XIV.

In the government of Britain the representatives of the people compose one branch of the national legislature. Commerce has been for ages the predominant pursuit of that country. Few nations, nevertheless, have been more frequently engaged in war; and the wars in which that kingdom has been engaged have, in numerous instances, proceeded from the people.

There have been, if I may so express it, almost as many popular as royal wars. The cries of the nation and the importunities of their representatives have, upon various occasions, dragged their monarchs into war, or continued them in it, contrary to their inclinations, and sometimes contrary to the real interests of the state. In that memorable struggle for superiority between the rival houses of *Austria* and *Bourbon*, which so long kept Europe in a flame, it is well known that the antipathies of the English against the French, seconding the ambition, or rather the avarice, of a favorite leader,[2] protracted the war beyond the limits marked out by sound policy, and for a considerable time in opposition to the views of the court.

The wars of these two last-mentioned nations have in a great

[1] The League of Cambray, comprehending the Emperor, the King of France, the King of Aragon, and most of the Italian princes and states.

[2] The Duke of Marlborough.

measure grown out of commercial considerations — the desire of supplanting and the fear of being supplanted, either in particular branches of traffic or in the general advantages of trade and navigation, and sometimes even the more culpable desire of sharing in the commerce of other nations without their consent.

The last war but two between Britain and Spain sprang from the attempts of the English merchants to prosecute an illicit trade with the Spanish main. These unjustifiable practices on their part produced severities on the part of the Spaniards towards the subjects of Great Britain which were not more justifiable, because they exceeded the bounds of a just retaliation and were chargeable with inhumanity and cruelty. Many of the English who were taken on the Spanish coasts were sent to dig in the mines of Potosi; and by the usual progress of a spirit of resentment the innocent were, after a while, confounded with the guilty in indiscriminate punishment. The complaints of the merchants kindled a violent flame throughout the nation, which soon after broke out in the House of Commons, and was communicated from that body to the ministry. Letters of reprisal were granted, and a war ensued, which in its consequences overthrew all the alliances that but twenty years before had been formed with sanguine expectations of the most beneficial fruits.

From this summary of what has taken place in other countries, whose situations have borne the nearest resemblance to our own, what reason can we have to confide in those reveries which would seduce us into an expectation of peace and cordiality between the members of the present confederacy, in a state of separation? Have we not already seen enough of the fallacy and extravagance of those idle theories which have amused us with promises of an exemption from the imperfections, the weaknesses, and the evils incident to society in every shape? Is it not time to awake from the deceitful dream of a golden age, and to adopt as a practical maxim for the direction of our political conduct that we, as well as the other inhabitants of the globe, are yet remote from the happy empire of perfect wisdom and perfect virtue?

Let the point of extreme depression to which our national dignity and credit have sunk, let the inconveniences felt everywhere from a lax and ill administration of government, let the revolt of a part of the state of North Carolina, the late menacing disturbances in Pennsylvania, and the actual insurrections and rebellions in Massachusetts, declare!

So far is the general sense of mankind from corresponding with the tenets of those who endeavor to lull asleep our apprehensions of discord and hostility between the states, in the event of disunion, that it has from long observation of the progress of society become a sort of axiom in politics, that vicinity, or nearness of situation, constitutes nations natural enemies. An intelligent writer expresses himself on this subject to this effect: "NEIGHBORING NATIONS [says he] are naturally ENEMIES of each other, unless their common weakness forces them to league in a CONFEDERATIVE REPUBLIC, and their constitution prevents the differences that neighborhood occasions, extinguishing that secret jealousy which disposes all states to aggrandize themselves at the expense of their neighbors."[1] This passage, at the same time, points out the EVIL and suggests the REMEDY. PUBLIUS.

THE SUBJECT CONTINUED, AND PARTICULAR CAUSES ENUMERATED[2]

It is sometimes asked, with an air of seeming triumph, what inducements could the states have, if disunited, to make war upon each other? It would be a full answer to this question to say — precisely the same inducements which have, at different times, deluged in blood all the nations in the world. But, unfortunately for us, the question admits of a more particular answer. There are causes of difference within our immediate contemplation, of the tendency of which, even under the restraints of a federal constitution, we have had sufficient experience to enable us to form a judgment of what might be expected if those restraints were removed.

[1] Vide *Principes des Négociations*, par l'Abbé de Mably.
[2] No. VII. Hamilton. Independent Journal, November 17, 1787.

Territorial disputes have at all times been found one of the most fertile sources of hostility among nations. Perhaps the greatest proportion of the wars that have desolated the earth have sprung from this origin. This cause would exist among us in full force. We have a vast tract of unsettled territory within the boundaries of the United States. There still are discordant and undecided claims between several of them, and the dissolution of the Union would lay a foundation for similar claims between them all. It is well known that they have heretofore had serious and animated discussions concerning the right to the lands which were ungranted at the time of the Revolution, and which usually went under the name of crown lands. The states within the limits of whose colonial governments they were comprised have claimed them as their property, the others have contended that the rights of the crown in this article devolved upon the Union; especially as to all that part of the Western territory which, either by actual possession, or through the submission of the Indian proprietors, was subjected to the jurisdiction of the king of Great Britain, till it was relinquished in the treaty of peace. This, it has been said, was at all events an acquisition to the Confederacy by compact with a foreign power. It has been the prudent policy of Congress to appease this controversy, by prevailing upon the states to make cessions to the United States for the benefit of the whole. This has been so far accomplished as, under a continuation of the Union, to afford a decided prospect of an amicable termination of the dispute. A dismemberment of the Confederacy, however, would revive this dispute, and would create others on the same subject. At present, a large part of the vacant Western territory is, by cession at least, if not by any anterior right, the common property of the Union. If that were at an end, the states which have made cessions, on a principle of federal compromise, would be apt, when the motive of the grant had ceased, to reclaim the lands as a reversion. The other states would no doubt insist on a proportion, by right of representation. Their argument would be that a grant, once made, could not be revoked; and that the justice of their participating in territory acquired or secured by the joint efforts of the Confederacy, remained undiminished. If, contrary to probability, it should be admitted by all the states that each had a right to a share of this common stock, there would still be a difficulty to be surmounted, as to a proper rule of apportionment. Different principles would be set up by different states for this purpose, and as they would affect the opposite interests of the parties, they might not easily be susceptible of a pacific adjustment.

In the wide field of Western territory, therefore, we perceive an ample theater for hostile pretensions, without any umpire or common judge to interpose between the contending parties. To reason from the past to the future, we shall have good ground to apprehend that the sword would sometimes be appealed to as the arbiter of their differences. The circumstances of the dispute between Connecticut and Pennsylvania, respecting the lands at Wyoming, admonish us not to be sanguine in expecting an easy accommodation of such differences. The Articles of Confederation obliged the parties to submit the matter to the decision of a federal court. The submission was made, and the court decided in favor of Pennsylvania. But Connecticut gave strong indications of dissatisfaction with that determination; nor did she appear to be entirely resigned to it, till, by negotiation and management, something like an equivalent was found for the loss she supposed herself to have sustained. Nothing here said is intended to convey the slightest censure on the conduct of that state. She no doubt sincerely believed herself to have been injured by the decision; and states, like individuals, acquiesce with great reluctance in determinations to their disadvantage.

Those who had an opportunity of seeing the inside of the transactions which attended the progress of the controversy between this state and the district of Vermont, can vouch the opposition we experienced, as well from states not interested as from those which were interested in the claim; and can attest the danger to which the peace of the Confederacy might have been exposed, had this state attempted to assert its rights by force. Two motives preponderated in that opposition: one, a jealousy entertained of our future power; and the other, the interest of certain individuals of influence in the neighboring states, who had obtained grants of lands under the actual government of that district. Even the states which brought forward claims in contradiction to ours, seemed more solicitous to dismember this state than to establish their own pretensions. These were New Hampshire, Massachusetts, and Connecticut. New Jersey and Rhode Island, upon all occasions, discovered a warm zeal for the independence of Vermont; and Maryland, until alarmed by the appearance of a connection between Canada and that place, entered deeply into the same views. These, being small states, saw with an unfriendly eye the perspective of our growing greatness. In a review of these transactions we may trace some of the causes which would be likely to embroil the states with each other, if it should be their unpropitious destiny to become disunited.

The competitions of commerce would be another fruitful source of contention. The states less favorably circumstanced would be desirous of escaping from the disadvantages of local situation, and of sharing in the advantages of their more fortunate neighbors. Each state, or separate confederacy, would pursue a system of commercial polity peculiar to itself. This would occasion distinctions, preferences, and exclusions, which would beget discontent. The habits of intercourse, on the basis of equal privileges, to which we have been accustomed from the earliest settlement of the country, would give a keener edge to those causes of discontent than they would naturally have independent of this circumstance. *We should be ready to denominate injuries those things which were in reality the justifiable acts of independent sovereignties consulting a distinct interest.* The spirit of enterprise, which characterizes the commercial part of America, has left no occasion of displaying itself unimproved. It is not at all probable that this unbridled spirit would pay much respect to those regulations of trade by which particular states might endeavor to secure exclusive benefits to their own citizens. The infractions of these regulations on one side, the efforts to prevent and repel them on the other, would naturally lead to outrages, and these to reprisals and wars.

The opportunities which some states would have of rendering others tributary to them by commercial regulations would be impatiently submitted to by the tributary states. The relative situation of New York, Connecticut, and New Jersey would afford an example of this kind. New York, from the necessities of revenue, must lay duties on her importations. A great part of these duties must be paid by the inhabitants of the two other states in the capacity of consumers of what we import. New York would neither be willing nor able to forego this advantage. Her citizens would not consent that a duty paid by them should be remitted in favor of the citizens of her neighbors; nor would it be practicable, if there were not this impediment in the way, to distinguish the customers in our own markets. Would Connecticut and New Jersey long submit to be taxed by New York for her exclusive benefit? Should we be long permitted to remain in the quiet and undisturbed enjoyment of a metropolis, from the possession of which we derived an advantage so odious to our neighbors, and, in their opinion, so oppressive? Should we be able to preserve it against the incumbent weight of Connecticut on the one side, and the coöperating pressure of New Jersey on the other? These are questions that temerity alone will answer in the affirmative.

The public debt of the Union would be a further cause of collision between the separate states or confederacies. The apportionment, in the first instance, and the progressive extinguishment afterwards, would be alike productive of ill-humor and animosity. How would it be possible to agree upon a rule of apportionment satisfactory to all? There is scarcely any that can be proposed which is entirely free from real objections. These, as usual, would be exaggerated by the adverse interests of the parties. There are even dissimilar views among the states as to the general principle of discharging the public debt. Some of them, either less impressed with the importance of national credit, or because their citizens have little, if any, immediate interest in the question, feel an indifference, if not a repugnance, to the payment of the domestic debt at any rate. These would be inclined to magnify the difficulties of a distribution. Others of them, a numerous body of whose citizens are creditors to the public beyond the proportion of the state in the total amount of the national debt, would be strenuous for some equitable and effectual provision. The procrastinations of the former would excite the resentments of the latter. The settlement of a rule would, in the meantime, be postponed by real differences of opinion and affected delays. The citizens of the states interested would clamor; foreign powers would urge for the satisfaction of their just demands, and the peace of the states would be hazarded to the double contingency of external invasion and internal contention.

Suppose the difficulties of agreeing upon a rule surmounted, and the apportionment made. Still there is great room to suppose that the rule agreed upon would, upon experiment, be found to bear harder upon some states than upon others. Those which were sufferers by it would naturally seek for a mitigation of the burden. The others would as naturally be disinclined to a revision, which was likely to end in an increase of their own incumbrances. Their refusal would be too plausible a pretext to the complaining states to withhold their contributions, not to be embraced with avidity; and the non-compliance of these states with their engagements would be a ground of bitter dissension and altercation. If even the rule adopted should in practice justify the equality of its principle, still delinquencies in payment on the part of some of the states would result from a diversity of other causes — the real deficiency of resources; the mismanagement of their finances; accidental disorders in the administration of the government, and, in addition to the rest, the reluctance with which men commonly part with money for purposes that have outlived the exigencies which produced them, and interfere with the supply of immediate wants. Delinquencies, from whatever causes, would be productive of complaints, recriminations, and quarrels. There is, perhaps, nothing more likely to disturb the tranquillity of nations than their being bound to mutual contributions for any common object which does not yield an equal and coincident benefit. For it is an observation, as true as it is trite, that there is nothing men differ so readily about as the payment of money.

Laws in violation of private contracts, as they amount to aggressions on the rights of those states whose citizens are injured by them, may be considered as another probable source of hostility. We are not authorized to expect that a more liberal or more equitable spirit would preside over the legislations of the individual states hereafter, if unrestrained by any additional checks, than we have heretofore seen in too many instances disgracing their several codes. We have observed the disposition to retaliation excited in Connecticut, in consequence of the enormities perpetrated by the legislature of Rhode Island; and we may reasonably infer that, in similar cases under other circumstances, a war, not of *parchment*, but of the sword, would chastise such atrocious breaches of moral obligation and social justice.

The probability of incompatible alliances between the different states or confederacies and different foreign nations, and the effects of this situation upon the peace of the whole, have been sufficiently unfolded in some preceding papers. From the view they have exhibited of this part of the subject, this conclusion is to be drawn, that America, if not connected at all, or only by the feeble tie of a simple league, offensive and defensive, would, by the operation of such opposite and jarring alliances, be gradually entangled in all the pernicious labyrinths of European politics and wars; and by the destructive contentions of the parts into which she was divided, would be likely to become a prey to the artifices and machinations of powers equally the enemies of them all. *Divide et impera* [1] must be the motto of every nation that either hates or fears us. PUBLIUS.

[1] Divide and command.

The Effects of Internal War in producing standing Armies and other Institutions unfriendly to Liberty[1]

Assuming it therefore as an established truth that the several states, in case of disunion, or such combinations of them as might happen to be formed out of the wreck of the general confederacy, would be subject to those vicissitudes of peace and war, of friendship and enmity with each other, which have fallen to the lot of all neighboring nations not united under one government, let us enter into a concise detail of some of the consequences that would attend such a situation.

War between the states, in the first periods of their separate existence, would be accompanied with much greater distresses than it commonly is in those countries where regular military establishments have long obtained. The disciplined armies always kept on foot on the continent of Europe, though they bear a malignant aspect to liberty and economy, have, notwithstanding, been productive of the signal advantage of rendering sudden conquests impracticable, and of preventing that rapid desolation which used to mark the progress of war prior to their introduction. The art of fortification has contributed to the same ends. The nations of Europe are encircled with chains of fortified places, which mutually obstruct invasion. Campaigns are wasted in reducing two or three frontier garrisons, to gain admittance into an enemy's country. Similar impediments occur at every step, to exhaust the strength and delay the progress of an invader. Formerly, an invading army would penetrate into the heart of a neighboring country almost as soon as intelligence of its approach could be received; but now a comparatively small force of disciplined troops, acting on the defensive, with the aid of posts, is able to impede, and finally to frustrate, the enterprises of one much more considerable. The history of war, in that quarter of the globe, is no longer a history of nations subdued and empires overturned; but of

[1] No. VIII. Hamilton. New York Packet, November 20, 1787.

towns taken and retaken, of battles that decide nothing, of retreats more beneficial than victories, of much effort and little acquisition.

In this country the scene would be altogether reversed. The jealousy of military establishments would postpone them as long as possible. The want of fortifications, leaving the frontiers of one state open to another, would facilitate inroads. The populous states would, with little difficulty, overrun their less populous neighbors. Conquests would be as easy to be made as difficult to be retained. War, therefore, would be desultory and predatory. Plunder and devastation ever march in the train of irregulars. The calamities of individuals would make the principal figure in the events which would characterize our military exploits.

This picture is not too highly wrought; though, I confess, it would not long remain a just one. Safety from external danger is the most powerful director of national conduct. Even the ardent lover of liberty will, after a time, give way to its dictates. The violent destruction of life and property incident to war, the continual effort and alarm attendant on a state of continual danger, will compel nations the most attached to liberty to resort for repose and security to institutions which have a tendency to destroy their civil and political rights. To be more safe, they at length become willing to run the risk of being less free.

The institutions chiefly alluded to are STANDING ARMIES and the correspondent appendages of military establishment. Standing armies, it is said, are not provided against in the new Constitution; and it is thence inferred that they would exist under it.[1] This inference, from the very form of the proposition, is, at best, problematical and uncertain. But standing armies, it may be replied, must inevitably result from a dissolution of

[1] This objection will be fully examined in its proper place, and it will be shown that the only rational precaution which could have been taken on this subject has been taken, and a much better one than is to be found in any constitution that has been heretofore framed in America, most of which contain no guard at all on this subject.

the confederacy. Frequent war and constant apprehension, which require a state of as constant preparation, will infallibly produce them. The weaker states or confederacies would first have recourse to them, to put themselves upon an equality with their more potent neighbors. They would endeavor to supply the inferiority of population and resources by a more regular and effective system of defense, by disciplined troops, and by fortifications. They would, at the same time, be necessitated to strengthen the executive arm of government, in doing which their constitutions would acquire a progressive direction towards monarchy. It is of the nature of war to increase the executive at the expense of the legislative authority.

The expedients which have been mentioned would soon give the states or confederacies that made use of them a superiority over their neighbors. Small states, or states of less natural strength, under vigorous governments, and with the assistance of disciplined armies, have often triumphed over large states, or states of greater natural strength, which have been destitute of these advantages. Neither the pride nor the safety of the more important states or confederacies would permit them long to submit to this mortifying and adventitious inferiority. They would quickly resort to means similar to those by which it had been effected, to reinstate themselves in their lost preëminence. Thus we should, in a little time, see established in every part of this country the same engines of despotism which have been the scourge of the Old World. This, at least, would be the natural course of things; and our reasonings will be the more likely to be just, in proportion as they are accommodated to this standard.

These are not vague inferences drawn from supposed or speculative defects in a constitution, the whole power of which is lodged in the hands of the people, or their representatives and delegates, but they are solid conclusions, drawn from the natural and necessary progress of human affairs.

It may, perhaps, be asked, by way of objection to this, why did not standing armies spring up out of the contentions which so often distracted the ancient republics of Greece? Different answers, equally satisfactory, may be given to this question. The industrious habits of the people of the present day, absorbed in the pursuits of gain, and devoted to the improvements of agriculture and commerce, are incompatible with the condition of a nation of soldiers, which was the true condition of the people of those republics. The means of revenue, which have been so greatly multiplied by the increase of gold and silver and of the arts of industry, and the science of finance, which is the offspring of modern times, concurring with the habits of nations, have produced an entire revolution in the system of war, and have rendered disciplined armies, distinct from the body of the citizens, the inseparable companions of frequent hostility.

There is a wide difference, also, between military establishments in a country seldom exposed by its situation to internal invasions, and in one which is often subject to them, and always apprehensive of them. The rulers of the former can have no good pretext, if they are even so inclined, to keep on foot armies so numerous as must of necessity be maintained in the latter. These armies being, in the first case, rarely, if at all, called into activity for interior defense, the people are in no danger of being broken to military subordination. The laws are not accustomed to relaxations, in favor of military exigencies; the civil state remains in full vigor, neither corrupted, nor confounded with the principles or propensities of the other state. The smallness of the army renders the natural strength of the community an over-match for it; and the citizens, not habituated to look up to the military power for protection, or to submit to its oppressions, neither love nor fear the soldiery; they view them with a spirit of jealous acquiescence in a necessary evil, and stand ready to resist a power which they suppose may be exerted to the prejudice of their rights. The army under such circumstances may usefully aid the magistrate to suppress a small faction, or an occasional mob, or insurrection; but it will be unable to enforce encroachments against the united efforts of the great body of the people.

In a country in the predicament last described, the contrary of all this happens. The perpetual menacings of danger oblige the government to be always prepared to repel it; its armies must be numerous enough for instant defense. The continual necessity for their services enhances the importance of the soldier, and proportionally degrades the condition of the citizen. The military state becomes elevated above the civil. The inhabitants of territories, often the theater of war, are unavoidably subjected to frequent infringements on their rights, which serve to weaken their sense of those rights; and by degrees the people are brought to consider the soldiery not only as their protectors but as their superiors. The transition from this disposition to that of considering them as masters, is neither remote nor difficult; but it is very difficult to prevail upon a people under such impressions, to make a bold or effectual resistance to usurpations supported by the military power.

The kingdom of Great Britain falls within the first description. An insular situation, and a powerful marine, guarding it in a great measure against the possibility of foreign invasion, supersede the necessity of a numerous army within the kingdom. A sufficient force to make head against a sudden descent, till the militia could have time to rally and embody, is all that has been deemed requisite. No motive of national policy has demanded, nor would public opinion have tolerated, a larger number of troops upon its domestic establishment. There has been, for a long time past, little room for the operation of the other causes, which have been enumerated as the consequences of internal war. This peculiar felicity of situation has, in a great degree, contributed to preserve the liberty which that country to this day enjoys, in spite of the prevalent venality and corruption. If, on the contrary, Britain had been situated on the continent, and had been compelled, as she would have been, by that situation, to make her military establishments at home coextensive with those of the other great powers of Europe, she, like them, would in all probability be, at this day, a victim to the absolute power of a single man. 'Tis possible, though not easy, that the people of that island may be enslaved from other causes; but it cannot be by the prowess of an army so inconsiderable as that which has been usually kept up within the kingdom.

If we are wise enough to preserve the Union we may for ages enjoy an advantage similar to that of an insulated situation. Europe is at a great distance from us. Her colonies in our vicinity will be likely to continue too much disproportioned in strength to be able to give us any dangerous annoyance. Extensive military establishments cannot, in this position, be necessary to our security. But if we should be disunited, and the integral parts should either remain separated, or, which is most probable, should be thrown together into two or three confederacies, we should be, in a short course of time, in the predicament of the continental powers of Europe — our liberties would be a prey to the means of defending ourselves against the ambition and jealousy of each other.

This is an idea not superficial nor futile, but solid and weighty. It deserves the most serious and mature consideration of every prudent and honest man of whatever party. If such men will make a firm and solemn pause, and meditate dispassionately on the importance of this interesting idea; if they will contemplate it in all its attitudes, and trace it to all its consequences, they will not hesitate to part with trival objections to a Constitution, the rejection of which would in all probability put a final period to the Union. The airy phantoms that flit before the distempered imaginations of some of its adversaries would quickly give place to the more substantial prospects of dangers, real, certain, and formidable.

PUBLIUS.

II

THE NEED OF A STRONG FEDERATION

(*a*) TO PREVENT INTERNAL STRIFE

The Utility of the Union as a Safeguard against Domestic Faction and Insurrection[1]

A firm union will be of the utmost moment to the peace and liberty of the states, as a barrier against domestic faction and insurrection. It is impossible to read the history of the petty republics of Greece and Italy without feeling sensations of horror and disgust at the distractions with which they were continually agitated, and at the rapid succession of revolutions by which they were kept in a state of perpetual vibration between the extremes of tyranny and anarchy. If they exhibit occasional calms, these only serve as short-lived contrasts to the furious storms that are to succeed. If now and then intervals of felicity open themselves to view, we behold them with a mixture of regret, arising from the reflection that the pleasing scenes before us are soon to be overwhelmed by the tempestuous waves of sedition and party rage. If momentary rays of glory break forth from the gloom, while they dazzle us with a transient and fleeting brilliancy, they at the same time admonish us to lament that the vices of government should pervert the direction and tarnish the luster of those bright talents and exalted endowments for which the favored soils that produced them have been so justly celebrated.

From the disorders that disfigure the annals of those republics the advocates of despotism have drawn arguments, not only against the forms of republican government, but against the very principles of civil liberty. They have decried all free govern-

[1] No. IX. Hamilton. Independent Journal, November 21, 1787.

ment as inconsistent with the order of society, and have indulged themselves in malicious exultation over its friends and partisans. Happily for mankind, stupendous fabrics reared on the basis of liberty, which have flourished for ages, have, in a few glorious instances, refuted their gloomy sophisms. And, I trust, America will be the broad and solid foundation of other edifices, not less magnificent, which will be equally permanent monuments of their errors.

But it is not to be denied that the portraits they have sketched of republican government were too just copies of the originals from which they were taken. If it had been found impracticable to have devised models of a more perfect structure, the enlightened friends to liberty would have been obliged to abandon the cause of that species of government as indefensible. The science of politics, however, like most other sciences, has received great improvement. The efficacy of various principles is now well understood, which were either not known at all, or imperfectly known to the ancients. The regular distribution of power into distinct departments; the introduction of legislative balances and checks; the institution of courts composed of judges holding their offices during good behavior; the representation of the people in the legislature by deputies of their own election: these are either wholly new discoveries, or have made their principal progress towards perfection in modern times. They are means, and powerful means, by which the excellencies of republican government may be retained and its imperfections lessened or avoided. To this catalogue of circumstances that tend to the amelioration of popular systems of civil government, I shall venture, however novel it may appear to some, to add one more, on a principle which has been made the foundation of an objection to the new Constitution: I mean the ENLARGEMENT of the ORBIT within which such systems are to revolve, either in respect to the dimensions of a single state, or to the consolidation of several smaller states into one great confederacy. The latter is that which immediately concerns the object under consideration. It will, however, be of use to examine the principle in its application to a single state, which shall be attended to in another place.

The utility of a confederacy as well to suppress faction and to guard the internal tranquillity of states, as to increase their external force and security, is in reality not a new idea. It has been practiced upon in different countries and ages, and has received the sanction of the most applauded writers on the subjects of politics. The opponents of the PLAN proposed have, with great assiduity, cited and circulated the observations of Montesquieu on the necessity of a contracted territory for a republican government. But they seem not to have been apprised of the sentiments of that great man expressed in another part of his work, nor to have adverted to the consequences of the principle to which they subscribe with such ready acquiescence.

When Montesquieu recommends a small extent for republics, the standards he had in view were of dimensions far short of the limits of almost every one of these states. Neither Virginia, Massachusetts, Pennsylvania, New York, North Carolina, nor Georgia can by any means be compared with the models from which he reasoned and to which the terms of his description apply. If we therefore take his ideas on this point as the criterion of truth, we shall be driven to the alternative either of taking refuge at once in the arms of monarchy, or of splitting ourselves into an infinity of little, jealous, clashing, tumultuous commonwealths, the wretched nurseries of unceasing discord, and the miserable objects of universal pity or contempt. Some of the writers who have come forward on the other side of the question seem to have been aware of the dilemma; and have even been bold enough to hint at the division of the larger states as a desirable thing. Such an infatuated policy, such a desperate expedient, might, by the multiplication of petty offices, answer the views of men who possess not qualifications to extend their influence beyond the narrow circles of personal intrigue, but it could never promote the greatness or happiness of the people of America.

Referring the examination of the principle itself to another place, as has been already mentioned, it will be sufficient to remark here that, in the sense of the author who has been most emphatically quoted upon the occasion, it would only dictate a reduction of the SIZE of the more considerable MEMBERS of the Union, but would not militate against their being all comprehended in one confederate government. And this is the true question, in the discussion of which we are at present interested.

So far are the suggestions of Montesquieu from standing in opposition to a general Union of the states, that he explicitly treats of a CONFEDERATE REPUBLIC as the expedient for extending the sphere of popular government, and reconciling the advantages of monarchy with those of republicanism.

"It is very probable" (says he [1]) "that mankind would have been obliged, at length, to live constantly under the government of a SINGLE PERSON, had they not contrived a kind of constitution that has all the internal advantages of a republican, together with the external force of a monarchical, government. I mean a CONFEDERATE REPUBLIC.

"This form of government is a convention, by which several smaller *states* agree to become members of a larger *one*, which they intend to form. It is a kind of assemblage of societies that constitute a new one, capable of increasing, by means of new associations, till they arrive to such a degree of power as to be able to provide for the security of the united body.

"A republic of this kind, able to withstand an external force, may support itself without any internal corruption. The form of this society prevents all manner of inconveniences.

"If a single member should attempt to usurp the supreme authority, he could not be supposed to have an equal authority and credit in all the confederate states. Were he to have too great influence over one, this would alarm the rest. Were he to subdue a part, that which would still remain free might oppose him with forces independent of those which he had usurped, and overpower him before he could be settled in his usurpation.

"Should a popular insurrection happen in one of the con-

[1] *Spirit of Laws*, vol. i, book ix, chap. 1.

federate states, the others are able to quell it. Should abuses creep into one part, they are reformed by those that remain sound. The state may be destroyed on one side, and not on the other; the confederacy may be dissolved, and the confederates preserve their sovereignty.

"As this government is composed of small republics it enjoys the internal happiness of each; and with respect to its external situation, it is possessed, by means of the association, of all the advantages of large monarchies."

I have thought it proper to quote at length these interesting passages, because they contain a luminous abridgment of the principal arguments in favor of the Union, and must effectually remove the false impressions which a misapplication of other parts of the work was calculated to produce. They have, at the same time, an intimate connection with the more immediate design of this paper; which is to illustrate the tendency of the Union to repress domestic faction and insurrection.

A distinction, more subtle than accurate, has been raised between a *confederacy* and a *consolidation* of the states. The essential characteristic of the first is said to be the restriction of its authority to the members in their collective capacities, without reaching to the individuals of whom they are composed. It is contended that the national council ought to have no concern with any object of internal administration. An exact equality of suffrage between the members has also been insisted upon as a leading feature of a confederate government. These positions are, in the main, arbitrary; they are supported neither by principle nor precedent. It has indeed happened that governments of this kind have generally operated in the manner which the distinction, taken notice of, supposes to be inherent in their nature; but there have been in most of them extensive exceptions to the practice, which serve to prove, as far as example will go, that there is no absolute rule on the subject. And it will be clearly shown, in the course of this investigation, that as far as the principle contended for has prevailed, it has been the cause of incurable disorder and imbecility in the government.

The definition of a *confederate republic* seems simply to be "an assemblage of societies," or an association of two or more states into one state. The extent, modifications, and objects of the federal authority are mere matters of discretion. So long as the separate organization of the members be not abolished, so long as it exists, by a constitutional necessity, for local purposes, though it should be in perfect subordination to the general authority of the Union, it would still be, in fact and in theory, an association of states, or a confederacy. The proposed Constitution, so far from implying an abolition of the state governments, makes them constituent parts of the national sovereignty, by allowing them a direct representation in the Senate, and leaves in their possession certain exclusive and very important portions of sovereign power. This fully corresponds, in every rational import of the terms, with the idea of a federal government.

In the Lycian Confederacy, which consisted of twenty-three CITIES or republics, the largest were entitled to *three* votes in the COMMON COUNCIL, those of the middle class to *two*, and the smallest to *one*. The COMMON COUNCIL had the appointment of all the judges and magistrates of the respective CITIES. This was certainly the most delicate species of interference in their internal administration; for if there be anything that seems exclusively appropriated to the local jurisdictions, it is the appointment of their own officers. Yet Montesquieu, speaking of this association, says: "Were I to give a model of an excellent confederate republic, it would be that of Lycia." Thus we perceive that the distinctions insisted upon were not within the contemplation of this enlightened civilian; and we shall be led to conclude that they are the novel refinements of an erroneous theory.

PUBLIUS.

THE SAME SUBJECT CONTINUED[1]

Among the numerous advantages promised by a well-constructed union, none deserves to be more accurately developed than its tendency to break and control the violence of faction. The friend of popular governments never finds himself so much alarmed for their character and fate as when he contemplates their propensity to this dangerous vice. He will not fail, therefore, to set a due value on any plan which, without violating the principles to which he is attached, provides a proper cure for it. The instability, injustice, and confusion introduced into the public councils, have, in truth, been the mortal diseases under which popular governments have everywhere perished, as they continue to be the favorite and fruitful topics from which the adversaries to liberty derive their most specious declamations. The valuable improvements made by the American constitutions on the popular models, both ancient and modern, cannot certainly be too much admired; but it would be an unwarrantable partiality to contend that they have as effectually obviated the danger on this side, as was wished and expected. Complaints are everywhere heard from our most considerate and virtuous citizens, equally the friends of public and private faith, and of public and personal liberty, that our governments are too unstable, that the public good is disregarded in the conflicts of rival parties, and that measures are too often decided, not according to the rules of justice and the rights of the minor party, but by the superior force of an interested and overbearing majority. However anxiously we may wish that these complaints had no foundations, the evidence of known facts will not permit us to deny that they are in some degree true. It will be found, indeed, on a candid review of our situation, that some of the distresses under which we labor have been erroneously charged on the operation of our governments; but it will be found, at the same time, that other causes will not alone account for many of our heaviest misfortunes,

[1] No. X. Madison. New York Daily Advertiser, November 22, 1787.

and, particularly, for that prevailing and increasing distrust of public engagements, and alarm for private rights, which are echoed from one end of the continent to the other. These must be chiefly, if not wholly, effects of the unsteadiness and injustice with which a factious spirit has tainted our public administration.

By a faction, I understand a number of citizens, whether amounting to a majority or minority of the whole, who are united and actuated by some common impulse of passion, or of interest, adverse to the rights of other citizens, or to the permanent and aggregate interests of the community.

There are two methods of curing the mischiefs of faction: the one, by removing its causes, the other, by controlling its effects.

There are again two methods of removing the causes of faction: the one, by destroying the liberty which is essential to its existence, the other, by giving to every citizen the same opinions, the same passions, and the same interests.

It could never be more truly said than of the first remedy, that it is worse than the disease. Liberty is to faction what air is to fire, an aliment without which it instantly expires. But it could not be a less folly to abolish liberty, which is essential to political life, because it nourishes faction, than it would be to wish the annihilation of air, which is essential to animal life, because it imparts to fire its destructive agency.

The second expedient is as impracticable as the first would be unwise. As long as the reason of man continues fallible, and he is at liberty to exercise it, different opinions will be formed. As long as the connection subsists between his reason and his self-love, his opinions and his passions will have a reciprocal influence on each other; and the former will be objects to which the latter will attach themselves. The diversity in the faculties of men, from which the rights of property originate, is not less an insuperable obstacle to an uniformity of interests. The protection of these faculties is the first object of government. From the protection of different and unequal faculties of acquiring property, the possession of different degrees and kinds of property immediately results; and from the influence of these on the sentiments and views of the respective proprietors, ensues a division of the society into different interests and parties.

The latent causes of faction are thus sown in the nature of man: and we see them everywhere brought into different degrees of activity, according to the different circumstances of civil society. A zeal for different opinions concerning religion, concerning government, and many other points, as well of speculation as of practice, an attachment to different leaders ambitiously contending for preëminence and power, or to persons of other descriptions whose fortunes have been interesting to the human passions, have, in turn, divided mankind into parties, inflamed them with mutual animosity, and rendered them much more disposed to vex and oppress each other than to coöperate for their common good. So strong is this propensity of mankind to fall into mutual animosities, that where no substantial occasion presents itself, the most frivolous and fanciful distinctions have been sufficient to kindle their unfriendly passions and excite their most violent conflicts. But the most common and durable source of factions has been the various and unequal distribution of property. Those who hold and those who are without property have ever formed distinct interests in society. Those who are creditors, and those who are debtors, fall under a like discrimination. A landed interest, a manufacturing interest, a mercantile interest, a moneyed interest, with many lesser interests, grow up of necessity in civilized nations, and divide them into different classes, actuated by different sentiments and views. The regulation of these various and interfering interests forms the principal task of modern legislation, and involves the spirit of party and faction in the necessary and ordinary operations of the government.

No man is allowed to be a judge in his own cause, because his interest would certainly bias his judgment, and, not improbably, corrupt his integrity. With equal, nay, with greater reason, a body of men are unfit to be both judges and parties at the same time; yet what are many of the most important acts of legislation but so many judicial determinations, not indeed concerning the rights of single persons, but concerning the rights of large bodies of citizens ? And what are the different classes of legislators but advocates and parties to the causes which they determine ? Is a law proposed concerning private debts ? It is a question to which the creditors are parties on one side and the debtors on the other. Justice ought to hold the balance between them. Yet the parties are, and must be, themselves the judges; and the most numerous party, or, in other words, the most powerful faction must be expected to prevail. Shall domestic manufactures be encouraged, and in what degree, by restrictions on foreign manufactures ? are questions which would be differently decided by the landed and the manufacturing classes, and probably by neither with a sole regard to justice and the public good. The apportionment of taxes on the various descriptions of property is an act which seems to require the most exact impartiality; yet there is, perhaps, no legislative act in which greater opportunity and temptation are given to a predominant party to trample on the rules of justice. Every shilling with which they overburden the inferior number is a shilling saved to their own pockets.

It is in vain to say that enlightened statesmen will be able to adjust these clashing interests, and render them all subservient to the public good. Enlightened statesmen will not always be at the helm; nor, in many cases, can such an adjustment be made at all without taking into view indirect and remote considerations, which will rarely prevail over the immediate interest which one party may find in disregarding the rights of another or the good of the whole.

The inference to which we are brought is that the *causes* of faction cannot be removed, and that relief is only to be sought in the means of controlling its *effects*.

If a faction consists of less than a majority, relief is supplied by the republican principle which enables the majority to defeat its sinister views by regular vote. It may clog the administration, it may convulse the society, but it will be unable to execute and mask its violence under the forms of the Constitution. When a majority is included in a faction, the form of popular government, on the other hand, enables it to sacrifice to its ruling passion or interest both the public good and the rights of other citizens. To secure the public good and private rights against the danger of such a faction, and at the same time to preserve the spirit and the form of popular government, is then the great object to which our inquiries are directed. Let me add that it is the great desideratum by which alone this form of government can be rescued from the opprobrium under which it has so long labored, and be recommended to the esteem and adoption of mankind.

By what means is this object attainable? Evidently by one of two only. Either the existence of the same passion or interest in a majority at the same time must be prevented, or the majority, having such coexistent passion or interest, must be rendered, by their number and local situation, unable to concert and carry into effect schemes of oppression. If the impulse and the opportunity be suffered to coincide, we well know that neither moral nor religious motives can be relied on as an adequate control. They are not found to be such on the injustice and violence of individuals, and lose their efficacy in proportion to the number combined together, that is, in proportion as their efficacy becomes needful.

From this view of the subject it may be concluded that a pure democracy, by which I mean a society consisting of a small number of citizens, who assemble and administer the government in person, can admit of no cure for the mischiefs of faction. A common passion or interest will, in almost every case, be felt by a majority of the whole; a communication and concert result from the form of government itself; and there is nothing to check the inducements to sacrifice the weaker party or an obnoxious individual. Hence it is that such democracies have ever been spectacles of turbulence and contention, have ever been found incompatible with personal security or the rights of property, and have in general been as short in their lives as they have been violent in their deaths. Theoretic politicians, who have patronized this species of government, have erroneously supposed that by reducing mankind to a perfect equality in their political rights, they would, at the same time, be perfectly equalized and assimilated in their possessions, their opinions, and their passions.

A republic, by which I mean a government in which the scheme of representation takes place, opens a different prospect, and promises the cure for which we are seeking. Let us examine the points in which it varies from pure democracy, and we shall comprehend both the nature of the cure and the efficacy which it must derive from the union.

The two great points of difference between a democracy and a republic are: first, the delegation of the government, in the latter, to a small number of citizens elected by the rest; secondly, the greater number of citizens, and greater sphere of country, over which the latter may be extended.

The effect of the first difference is, on the one hand, to refine and enlarge the public views by passing them through the medium of a chosen body of citizens, whose wisdom may best discern the true interest of their country, and whose patriotism and love of justice will be least likely to sacrifice it to temporary or partial considerations. Under such a regulation, it may well happen that the public voice, pronounced by the representatives of the people, will be more consonant to the public good than if pronounced by the people themselves, convened for the purpose. On the other hand, the effect may be inverted. Men of factious tempers, of local prejudices, or of sinister designs, may, by intrigue, by corruption, or by other means, first obtain the suffrages, and then betray the interests, of the people. The question resulting is, whether small or extensive republics are most favorable to the election of proper guardians of the public weal; and it is clearly decided in favor of the latter by two obvious considerations.

In the first place, it is to be remarked that, however small the republic may be, the representatives must be raised to a certain number, in order to guard against the cabals of a few; and that, however large it may be, they must be limited to a certain number, in order to guard against the confusion of a multitude. Hence the number of representatives in the two cases not being in proportion to that of the constituents, and being proportionally greatest in the small republic, it follows that, if the proportion of fit characters be not less in the large than in the small republic, the former will present a greater option, and consequently a greater probability of a fit choice.

In the next place, as each representative will be chosen by a greater number of citizens in the large than in the small republic, it will be more difficult for unworthy candidates to practice with success the vicious arts by which elections are too often carried; and the suffrages of the people being more free, will be more likely to center on men who possess the most attractive merit and the most diffusive and established characters.

It must be confessed that in this, as in most other cases, there is a mean, on both sides of which inconveniences will be found to lie. By enlarging too much the number of electors, you render the representative too little acquainted with all their local circumstances and lesser interests; as by reducing it too much, you render him unduly attached to these, and too little fit to comprehend and pursue great and national objects. The federal Constitution forms a happy combination in this respect; the great and aggregate interests being referred to the national, the local and particular to the state legislatures.

The other point of difference is the greater number of citizens and extent of territory which may be brought within the compass of republican than of democratic government; and it is this circumstance principally which renders factious combinations less to be dreaded in the former than in the latter. The smaller the society, the fewer probably will be the distinct parties and interests composing it; the fewer the distinct parties and interests, the more frequently will a majority be found of the same party; and the smaller the number of individuals composing a majority, and the smaller the compass within which they are placed, the more easily will they concert and execute their plans of oppression. Extend the sphere, and you take in a greater variety of parties and interests; you make it less probable that a majority of the whole will have a common motive to invade the rights of other citizens; or if such a common motive exists, it will be more difficult for all who feel it to discover their own strength, and to act in unison with each other. Besides other impediments, it may be remarked that, where there is a consciousness of unjust or dishonorable purposes, communication is always checked by distrust in proportion to the number whose concurrence is necessary.

Hence, it clearly appears, that the same advantage which a republic has over a democracy, in controlling the effects of faction, is enjoyed by a large over a small republic,— is enjoyed by the Union over the states composing it. Does this advantage consist in the substitution of representatives whose enlightened views and virtuous sentiments render them superior to local prejudices and to schemes of injustice? It will not be denied that the representation of the Union will be most likely to possess these requisite endowments. Does it consist in the greater security afforded by a greater variety of parties, against the event of any one party being able to outnumber and oppress the rest? In an equal degree does the increased variety of parties comprised within the Union increase this security? Does it, in fine, consist in the greater obstacles opposed to the concert and accomplishment of the secret wishes of an unjust and interested majority? Here, again, the extent of the Union gives it the most palpable advantage.

The influence of factious leaders may kindle a flame within their particular states, but will be unable to spread a general conflagration through the other states. A religious sect may degenerate into a political faction in a part of the Confederacy; but the variety of sects dispersed over the entire face of it must secure the national councils against any danger from that source.

A rage for paper money, for an abolition of debts, for an equal division of property, or for any other improper or wicked project, will be less apt to pervade the whole body of the Union than a particular member of it; in the same proportion as such a malady is more likely to taint a particular county or district, than an entire state.

In the extent and proper structure of the Union, therefore, we behold a republican remedy for the diseases most incident to republican government. And according to the degree of pleasure and pride we feel in being republicans, ought to be our zeal in cherishing the spirit and supporting the character of Federalists. PUBLIUS.

(*b*) TO DEVELOP AND PROTECT COMMERCE

THE UTILITY OF THE UNION IN RESPECT TO COMMERCE AND A NAVY [1]

The importance of the Union, in a commercial light, is one of those points about which there is least room to entertain a difference of opinion, and which has, in fact, commanded the most general assent of men who have any acquaintance with the subject. This applies as well to our intercourse with foreign countries as with each other.

There are appearances to authorize a supposition that the adventurous spirit, which distinguishes the commercial character of America, has already excited uneasy sensations in several of the maritime powers of Europe. They seem to be apprehensive of our too great interference in that carrying trade which is the support of their navigation and the foundation of their naval strength. Those of them which have colonies in America look forward to what this country is capable of becoming, with painful solicitude. They foresee the dangers that may threaten their American dominions from the neighborhood of states which have all the dispositions, and would possess all the means, requisite to the creation of a powerful marine. Impressions of

[1] No. XI. Hamilton. Independent Journal, November 24, 1787.

this kind will naturally indicate the policy of fostering divisions among us, and of depriving us, as far as possible, of an ACTIVE COMMERCE in our own bottoms. This would answer the threefold purpose of preventing our interference in their navigation, of monopolizing the profits of our trade, and of clipping the wings by which we might soar to a dangerous greatness. Did not prudence forbid the detail, it would not be difficult to trace, by facts, the workings of this policy to the cabinets of ministers.

If we continue united, we may counteract a policy so unfriendly to our prosperity in a variety of ways. By prohibitory regulations, extending, at the same time, throughout the states, we may oblige foreign countries to bid against each other for the privileges of our markets. This assertion will not appear chimerical to those who are able to appreciate the importance to any manufacturing nation of the markets of three millions of people — increasing in rapid progression, for the most part exclusively addicted to agriculture, and likely from local circumstances to remain in this disposition; and the immense difference there would be to the trade and navigation of such a nation, between a direct communication in its own ships, and an indirect conveyance of its products and returns, to and from America, in the ships of another country. Suppose, for instance, we had a government in America, capable of excluding Great Britain (with whom we have at present no treaty of commerce) from all our ports; what would be the probable operation of this step upon her politics? Would it not enable us to negotiate, with the fairest prospect of success, for commercial privileges of the most valuable and extensive kind, in the dominions of that kingdom? When these questions have been asked, upon other occasions, they have received a plausible, but not a solid or satisfactory answer. It has been said that prohibitions on our part would produce no change in the system of Britain, because she could prosecute her trade with us through the medium of the Dutch, who would be her immediate customers and paymasters for those articles which were wanted for the supply of our markets. But would not her navigation be materially injured by the loss of the important advantage of being her own carrier in that trade? Would not the principal part of its profits be intercepted by the Dutch, as a compensation for their agency and risk? Would not the mere circumstance of freight occasion a considerable deduction? Would not so circuitous an intercourse facilitate the competitions of other nations, by enhancing the price of British commodities in our markets, and by transferring to other hands the management of this interesting branch of the British commerce?

A mature consideration of the objects suggested by these questions will justify a belief that the real disadvantages to Great Britain from such a state of things, conspiring with the prepossessions of a great part of the nation in favor of the American trade, and with the importunities of the West India Islands, would produce a relaxation in her present system, and would let us into the enjoyment of privileges in the markets of those islands and elsewhere, from which our trade would derive the most substantial benefits. Such a point gained from the British government, and which could not be expected without an equivalent in exemptions and immunities in our markets, would be likely to have a correspondent effect on the conduct of other nations, who would not be inclined to see themselves altogether supplanted in our trade.

A further resource for influencing the conduct of European nations towards us in this respect would arise from the establishment of a federal navy. There can be no doubt that the continuance of the Union under an efficient government would put it in our power, at a period not very distant, to create a navy which, if it could not vie with those of the great maritime powers, would at least be of respectable weight if thrown into the scale of either of two contending parties. This would be more particularly the case in relation to operations in the West Indies. A few ships of the line, sent opportunely to the reinforcement of either side, would often be sufficient to decide the fate of a campaign, on the event of which interests of the greatest magnitude were suspended. Our position is, in this respect, a very commanding one. And if to this consideration we add that of the usefulness of supplies from this country, in the prosecution of military operations in the West Indies, it will readily be perceived that a situation so favorable would enable us to bargain with great advantage for commercial privileges. A price would be set not only upon our friendship but upon our neutrality. By a steady adherence to the Union, we may hope, ere long, to become the arbiter of Europe in America, and to be able to incline the balance of European competitions in this part of the world as our interest may dictate.

But in the reverse of this eligible situation, we shall discover that the rivalships of the parts would make them checks upon each other, and would frustrate all the tempting advantages which nature has kindly placed within our reach. In a state so insignificant our commerce would be a prey to the wanton intermeddlings of all nations at war with each other; who, having nothing to fear from us, would with little scruple or remorse supply their wants by depredations on our property as often as it fell in their way. The rights of neutrality will only be respected when they are defended by an adequate power. A nation, despicable by its weakness, forfeits even the privilege of being neutral.

Under a vigorous national government, the natural strength and resources of the country, directed to a common interest, would baffle all the combinations of European jealousy to restrain our growth. This situation would even take away the motive to such combinations, by inducing an impracticability of success. An active commerce, an extensive navigation, a flourishing marine would then be the inevitable offspring of moral and physical necessity. We might defy the little arts of little politicans to control or vary the irresistible and unchangeable course of nature.

But in a state of disunion, these combinations might exist and might operate with success. It would be in the power of the maritime nations, availing themselves of our universal impotence, to prescribe the conditions of our political existence; and as they have a common interest in being our carriers, and still more in preventing our being theirs, they would in all probability combine to embarrass our navigation in such a manner as would in effect destroy it, and confine us to a PASSIVE COMMERCE. We should thus be compelled to content ourselves with the first price of our commodities, and to see the profits of our trade snatched from us to enrich our enemies and persecutors. That unequaled spirit of enterprise, which signalizes the genius of the American merchants and navigators, and which is in itself an inexhaustible mine of national wealth, would be stifled and lost, and poverty and disgrace would overspread a country which, with wisdom, might make herself the admiration and envy of the world.

There are rights of great moment to the trade of America which are rights of the Union — I allude to the fisheries, to the navigation of the Lakes, and to that of the Mississippi. The dissolution of the Confederacy would give room for delicate questions concerning the future existence of these rights, which the interest of more powerful partners would hardly fail to solve to our disadvantage. The disposition of Spain with regard to the Mississippi needs no comment. France and Britain are concerned with us in the fisheries, and view them as of the utmost moment to their navigation. They, of course, would hardly remain long indifferent to that decided mastery, of which experience has shown us to be possessed in this valuable branch of traffic, and by which we are able to undersell those nations in their own markets. What more natural than that they should be disposed to exclude from the lists such dangerous competitors?

This branch of trade ought not to be considered as a partial benefit. All the navigating states may, in different degrees, advantageously participate in it, and under circumstances of a greater extension of mercantile capital, would not be unlikely to do it. As a nursery of seamen, it now is, or, when time shall have more nearly assimilated the principles of navigation in the several states, will become, an universal resource. To the establishment of a navy, it must be indispensable.

To this great national object, a NAVY, union will contribute in various ways. Every institution will grow and flourish in proportion to the quantity and extent of the means concentered towards its formation and support. A navy of the United States, as it would embrace the resources of all, is an object far less remote than a navy of any single state or partial confederacy, which would only embrace the resources of a part. It happens, indeed, that different portions of confederated America possess each some peculiar advantage for this essential establishment. The more Southern States furnish in greater abundance certain kinds of naval stores — tar, pitch, and turpentine. Their wood for the construction of ships is also of a more solid and lasting texture. The difference in the duration of the ships of which the navy might be composed, if chiefly constructed of Southern wood, would be of signal importance, either in the view of naval strength or of national economy. Some of the Southern and of the Middle States yield a greater plenty of iron, and of better quality. Seamen must chiefly be drawn from the Northern hive. The necessity of naval protection to external or maritime commerce, and the conduciveness of that species of commerce to the prosperity of a navy, are points too manifest to require a particular elucidation. They, by a kind of reaction mutually beneficial, promote each other.

An unrestrained intercourse between the states themselves will advance the trade of each by an interchange of their respective productions, not only for the supply of reciprocal wants at home, but for exportation to foreign markets. The veins of commerce in every part will be replenished, and will acquire additional motion and vigor from a free circulation of the commodities of every part. Commercial enterprise will have much greater scope, from the diversity in the productions of different states. When the staple of one fails from a bad harvest or unproductive crop, it can call to its aid the staple of another. The variety, not less than the value, of products for exportation contributes to the activity of foreign commerce.

It can be conducted upon much better terms with a large number of materials of a given value than with a small number of materials of the same value, arising from the competitions of trade and from the fluctuations of markets. Particular articles may be in great demand at certain periods, and unsalable at others; but if there be a variety of articles, it can scarcely happen that they should all be at one time in the latter predicament, and on this account the operations of the merchant would be less liable to any considerable obstruction or stagnation. The speculative trader will at once perceive the force of these observations, and will acknowledge that the aggregate balance of the commerce of the United States would bid fair to be much more favorable than that of the thirteen states without union or with partial unions.

It may perhaps be replied to this, that whether the states are united or disunited, there would still be an intimate intercourse between them which would answer the same ends; but this intercourse would be fettered, interrupted, and narrowed by a multiplicity of causes which in the course of these papers have been amply detailed. An unity of commercial, as well as political, interests can only result from an unity of government.

There are other points of view in which this subject might be placed, of a striking and animating kind; but they would lead us too far into the regions of futurity, and would involve topics not proper for a newspaper discussion. I shall briefly observe that our situation invites and our interest prompts us to aim at an ascendant in the system of American affairs. The world may politically, as well as geographically, be divided into four parts, each having a distinct set of interests. Unhappily for the other three, Europe, by her arms and by her negotiations, by force and by fraud, has, in different degrees, extended her dominion over them all. Africa, Asia, and America have successively felt her domination. The superiority she has long maintained has tempted her to plume herself as the Mistress of the World, and to consider the rest of mankind as created for her benefit. Men admired as profound philosophers have, in direct terms, attributed to her inhabitants a physical superiority, and have gravely asserted that all animals, and with them the human species, degenerate in America — that even dogs cease to bark after having breathed awhile in our atmosphere.[1] Facts have too long supported these arrogant pretensions of the European. It belongs to us to vindicate the honor of the human race, and to teach that assuming brother, moderation. Union will enable us to do it. Disunion will add another victim to his triumphs. Let Americans disdain to be the instruments of European greatness! Let the thirteen states, bound together in a strict and indissoluble Union, concur in erecting one great American system, superior to the control of all transatlantic force or influence, and able to dictate the terms of the connection between the Old and the New World! PUBLIUS.

(c) TO PROVIDE AN ADEQUATE REVENUE

THE UTILITY OF THE UNION IN RESPECT TO REVENUE[2]

The effects of union, upon the commercial prosperity of the states, have been sufficiently delineated. Its tendency to promote the interests of revenue will be the subject of our present inquiry.

The prosperity of commerce is now perceived and acknowledged by all enlightened statesmen to be the most useful as well as the most productive source of national wealth, and has accordingly become a primary object of their political cares. By multiplying the means of gratification, by promoting the introduction and circulation of the precious metals, those darling objects of human avarice and enterprise, it serves to vivify and invigorate all the channels of industry, and to make them flow with greater activity and copiousness. The assiduous merchant, the laborious husbandman, the active mechanic, and the industrious manufacturer — all orders of men look forward with eager expectation and growing alacrity to this pleasing reward

[1] *Recherches philosophiques sur les Américains.*

[2] No. XII. Hamilton. New York Packet, November 27, 1787.

of their toils. The often-agitated question between agriculture and commerce has from indubitable experience received a decision which has silenced the rivalships that once subsisted between them, and has proved, to the entire satisfaction of their friends, that their interests are intimately blended and interwoven. It has been found, in various countries, that in proportion as commerce has flourished land has risen in value. And how could it have happened otherwise? Could that which procures a freer vent for the products of the earth — which furnishes new incitements to the cultivators of land — which is the most powerful instrument in increasing the quantity of money in a state — could that, in fine, which is the faithful handmaid of labor and industry, in every shape, fail to augment the value of that article, which is the prolific parent of far the greatest part of the objects upon which they are exerted? It is astonishing that so simple a truth should ever have had an adversary; and it is one, among a multitude of proofs, how apt a spirit of ill-informed jealousy or of too great abstraction and refinement is to lead men astray from the plainest paths of reason and conviction.

The ability of a country to pay taxes must always be proportioned, in a great degree, to the quantity of money in circulation and to the celerity with which it circulates. Commerce, contributing to both these objects, must of necessity render the payment of taxes easier, and facilitate the requisite supplies to the treasury. The hereditary dominions of the Emperor of Germany contain a great extent of fertile, cultivated and populous territory, a large proportion of which is situated in mild and luxuriant climates. In some parts of this territory are to be found the best gold and silver mines in Europe. And yet, from the want of the fostering influence of commerce, that monarch can boast but slender revenues. He has several times been compelled to owe obligations to the pecuniary succors of other nations for the preservation of his essential interests, and is unable, upon the strength of his own resources, to sustain a long or continued war.

But it is not in this aspect of the subject alone that union will be seen to conduce to the purposes of revenue. There are other points of view in which its influence will appear more immediate and decisive. It is evident from the state of the country, from the habits of the people, from the experience we have had on the point itself, that it is impracticable to raise any very considerable sums by direct taxation. Tax laws have in vain been multiplied; new methods to enforce the collection have in vain been tried; the public expectation has been uniformly disappointed, and the treasuries of the states have remained empty. The popular system of administration inherent in the nature of popular government, coinciding with the real scarcity of money incident to a languid and mutilated state of trade, has hitherto defeated every experiment for extensive collections, and has at length taught the different legislatures the folly of attempting them.

No person acquainted with what happens in other countries will be surprised at this circumstance. In so opulent a nation as that of Britain, where direct taxes from superior wealth must be much more tolerable, and, from the vigor of the government, much more practicable than in America, far the greatest part of the national revenue is derived from taxes of the indirect kind, from imposts, and from excises. Duties on imported articles form a large branch of this latter description.

In America, it is evident that we must a long time depend for the means of revenue chiefly on such duties. In most parts of it, excises must be confined within a narrow compass. The genius of the people will ill brook the inquisitive and peremptory spirit of excise laws. The pockets of the farmers, on the other hand, will reluctantly yield but scanty supplies, in the unwelcome shape of impositions on their houses and lands; and personal property is too precarious and invisible a fund to be laid hold of in any other way than by the imperceptible agency of taxes on consumption.

If these remarks have any foundation, that state of things which will best enable us to improve and extend so valuable a resource must be the best adapted to our political welfare. And it cannot admit of a serious doubt that this state of things must rest on the basis of a general union. As far as this would be conducive to the interests of commerce, so far it must tend to the extension of the revenue to be drawn from that source. As far as it would contribute to rendering regulations for the collection of the duties more simple and efficacious, so far it must serve to answer the purposes of making the same rate of duties more productive, and of putting it into the power of the government to increase the rate without prejudice to trade.

The relative situation of these states; the number of rivers with which they are intersected, and of bays that wash their shores; the facility of communication in every direction; the affinity of language and manners; the familiar habits of intercourse; — all these are circumstances that would conspire to render an illicit trade between them a matter of little difficulty, and would insure frequent evasions of the commercial regulations of each other. The separate states or confederacies would be necessitated by mutual jealousy to avoid the temptations to that kind of trade by the lowness of their duties. The temper of our governments, for a long time to come, would not permit those rigorous precautions by which the European nations guard the avenues into their respective countries, as well by land as by water; and which, even there, are found insufficient obstacles to the adventurous stratagems of avarice.

In France, there is an army of patrols (as they are called) constantly employed to secure her fiscal regulations against the inroads of the dealers in contraband. Mr. Neckar computes the number of these patrols at upwards of twenty thousand. This proves the immense difficulty in preventing that species of traffic, where there is an inland communication, and shows in a strong light the disadvantages with which the collection of duties in this country would be encumbered, if by disunion the states should be placed in a situation, with respect to each other, resembling that of France with respect to her neighbors. The arbitrary and vexatious powers with which the patrols are necessarily armed, would be intolerable in a free country.

If, on the contrary, there be but one government pervading all the states, there will be, as to the principal part of our commerce, but ONE SIDE to guard — the ATLANTIC COAST. Vessels arriving directly from foreign countries, laden with valuable cargoes, would rarely choose to hazard themselves to the complicated and critical perils which would attend attempts to unlade prior to their coming into port. They would have to dread both the dangers of the coast, and of detection, as well after as before their arrival at the places of their final destination. An ordinary degree of vigilance would be competent to the prevention of any material infractions upon the rights of the revenue. A few armed vessels, judiciously stationed at the entrances of our ports, might at small expense be made useful sentinels of the laws. And the government having the same interest to provide against violations everywhere, the coöperation of its measures in each state would have a powerful tendency to render them effectual. Here also we should preserve, by union, an advantage which nature holds out to us, and which would be relinquished by separation. The United States lie at a great distance from Europe, and at a considerable distance from all other places with which they would have extensive connections of foreign trade. The passage from them to us, in a few hours, or in a single night, as between the coasts of France and Britain, and of other neighboring nations, would be impracticable. This is a prodigious security against a direct contraband with foreign countries; but a circuitous contraband to one state, through the medium of another, would be both easy and safe. The difference between a direct importation from abroad, and an indirect importation through the channel of a neighboring state, in small parcels, according to time and opportunity, with the additional facilities of inland communication, must be palpable to every man of discernment.

It is therefore evident that one national government would be able, at much less expense, to extend the duties on imports, beyond comparison, further than would be practicable to the states separately, or to any partial confederacies. Hitherto, I believe, it may safely be asserted that these duties have not upon an average exceeded in any state three per cent. In France they are estimated at about fifteen per cent, and in Britain the proportion is still greater. There seems to be nothing to hinder their being increased in this country to at least treble their present amount. The single article of ardent spirits, under federal regulation, might be made to furnish a considerable revenue. Upon a ratio to the importation into this state, the whole quantity imported into the United States may at a low computation be estimated at four millions of gallons; which, at a shilling per gallon, would produce two hundred thousand pounds. That article would well bear this rate of duty; and if it should tend to diminish the consumption of it, such an effect would be equally favorable to the agriculture, to the economy, to the morals, and to the health of the society. There is, perhaps, nothing so much a subject of national extravagance as this very article.

What will be the consequence, if we are not able to avail ourselves of the resource in question in its full extent? A nation cannot long exist without revenue. Destitute of this essential support, it must resign its independence, and sink into the degraded condition of a province. This is an extremity to which no government will of choice accede. Revenue, therefore, must be had at all events. In this country, if the principal part be not drawn from commerce, it must fall with oppressive weight upon land. It has been already intimated that excises, in their true signification, are too little in unison with the feelings of the people to admit of great use being made of that mode of taxation; nor, indeed, in the states where almost the sole employment is agriculture, are the objects proper for excise sufficiently numerous to permit very ample collections in that way. Personal estate (as has been before remarked), from the difficulty in tracing it, cannot be subjected to large contributions by any other means than by taxes on consumption. In populous cities, it may be enough the subject of conjecture to occasion the oppression of individuals without much aggregate benefit to the state; but beyond these circles, it must, in a great measure, escape the eye and the hand of the tax-gatherer. As the necessities of the state, nevertheless, must be satisfied in some mode or other, the defect of other resources must throw the principal weight of the public burdens on the possessors of land. And as, on the other hand, the wants of the government can never obtain an adequate supply, unless all the sources of revenue are open to its demands, the finances of the community, under such embarrassments, cannot be put into a situation consistent with its respectability or its security. Thus we shall not even have the consolations of a full treasury to atone for the oppression of that valuable class of the citizens who are employed in the cultivation of the soil. But public and private distress will keep pace with each other in gloomy concert, and unite in deploring the infatuation of those counsels which led to disunion.

PUBLIUS.

THE SAME SUBJECT CONTINUED, WITH A VIEW TO ECONOMY[1]

As connected with the subject of revenue, we may with propriety consider that of economy. The money saved from one object may be usefully applied to another, and there will be so much the less to be drawn from the pockets of the people. If the states are united under one government, there will be but one national civil list to support; if they are divided into several confederacies, there will be as many different national civil lists to be provided for — and each of them, as to the principal departments, coextensive with that which would be necessary for a government of the whole. The entire separation of the states into thirteen unconnected sovereignties is a project too extravagant and too replete with danger to have many advocates. The ideas of men who speculate upon the dismemberment of the empire seem generally turned towards three confederacies —

[1] No. XIII. Hamilton. Independent Journal, November 28, 1787.

one consisting of the four Northern, another of the four Middle and a third of the five Southern States. There is little probability that there would be a greater number. According to this distribution, each confederacy would comprise an extent of territory larger than that of the kingdom of Great Britain. No well-informed man will suppose that the affairs of such a confederacy can be properly regulated by a government less comprehensive in its organs or institutions than that which has been proposed by the Convention. When the dimensions of a state attain to a certain magnitude, it requires the same energy of government and the same forms of administration which are requisite in one of much greater extent. This idea admits not of precise demonstration, because there is no rule by which we can measure the momentum of civil power necessary to the government of any given number of individuals; but when we consider that the island of Britain, nearly commensurate with each of the supposed confederacies, contains about eight millions of people, and when we reflect upon the degree of authority required to direct the passions of so large a society to the public good, we shall see no reason to doubt that the like portion of power would be sufficient to perform the same task in a society far more numerous. Civil power, properly organized and exerted, is capable of diffusing its force to a very great extent; and can, in a manner, reproduce itself in every part of a great empire by a judicious arrangement of subordinate institutions.

The supposition that each confederacy into which the states would be likely to be divided would require a government not less comprehensive than the one proposed, will be strengthened by another supposition more probable than that which presents us with three confederacies as the alternative to a general union. If we attend carefully to geographical and commercial considerations, in conjunction with the habits and prejudices of the different states, we shall be led to conclude that in case of disunion they will most naturally league themselves under two governments. The four Eastern States, from all the causes that form the links of national sympathy and connection, may with certainty be expected to unite. New York, situated as she is, would never be unwise enough to oppose a feeble and unsupported flank to the weight of that confederacy. There are obvious reasons that would facilitate her accession to it. New Jersey is too small a state to think of being a frontier, in opposition to this still more powerful combination; nor do there appear to be any obstacles to her admission into it. Even Pennsylvania would have strong inducements to join the Northern league. An active foreign commerce, on the basis of her own navigation, is her true policy, and coincides with the opinions and dispositions of her citizens. The more Southern states, from various circumstances, may not think themselves much interested in the encouragement of navigation. They may prefer a system which would give unlimited scope to all nations to be the carriers as well as the purchasers of their commodities. Pennsylvania may not choose to confound her interests in a connection so adverse to her policy. As she must at all events be a frontier, she may deem it most consistent with her safety to have her exposed side turned towards the weaker power of the Southern, rather than towards the stronger power of the Northern, confederacy. This would give her the fairest chance to avoid being the Flanders of America. Whatever may be the determination of Pennsylvania, if the Northern confederacy includes New Jersey, there is no likelihood of more than one confederacy to the south of that state.

Nothing can be more evident than that the thirteen states will be able to support a national government better than one half, or one third, or any number less than the whole. This reflection must have great weight in obviating that objection to the proposed plan, which is founded on the principle of expense; an objection, however, which, when we come to take a nearer view of it, will appear in every light to stand on mistaken ground.

If, in addition to the consideration of a plurality of civil lists, we take into view the number of persons who must necessarily be employed to guard the inland communication between the different confederacies against illicit trade, and who in time will infallibly spring up out of the necessities of revenue; and if we also take into view the military establishments which it has been shown would unavoidably result from the jealousies and conflicts of the several nations into which the states would be divided, we shall clearly discover that a separation would be not less injurious to the economy, than to the tranquillity, commerce, revenue, and liberty of every part.

PUBLIUS.

III

THE INADEQUACY OF THE OLD CONFEDERATION

(a) GENERAL FEATURES OF WEAKNESS

An Objection drawn from the Extent of Country answered[1]

We have seen the necessity of the Union, as our bulwark against foreign danger, as the conservator of peace among ourselves, as the guardian of our commerce and other common interests, as the only substitute for those military establishments which have subverted the liberties of the Old World, and as the proper antidote for the diseases of faction, which have proved fatal to other popular governments, and of which alarming symptoms have been betrayed by our own. All that remains, within this branch of our inquiries, is to take notice of an objection that may be drawn from the great extent of country which the Union embraces. A few observations on this subject will be the more proper, as it is perceived that the adversaries of the new Constitution are availing themselves of a prevailing prejudice with regard to the practicable sphere of republican administration, in order to supply, by imaginary difficulties, the want of those solid objections which they endeavor in vain to find.

The error which limits republican government to a narrow district has been unfolded and refuted in preceding papers. I remark here only that it seems to owe its rise and prevalence chiefly to the confounding of a republic with a democracy, applying to the former reasonings drawn from the nature of the latter. The true distinction between these forms was also adverted to on a former occasion. It is, that in a democracy the people meet and exercise the government in person; in a republic, they assemble and administer it by their representatives

[1] No. XIV. Madison. New York Packet, November 30, 1787.

and agents. A democracy, consequently, must be confined to a small spot. A republic may be extended over a large region.

To this accidental source of the error may be added the artifice of some celebrated authors, whose writings have had a great share in forming the modern standard of political opinions. Being subjects either of an absolute or limited monarchy, they have endeavored to heighten the advantages or palliate the evils of those forms, by placing in comparison with them the vices and defects of the republican, and by citing as specimens of the latter the turbulent democracies of ancient Greece and modern Italy. Under the confusion of names, it has been an easy task to transfer to a republic observations applicable to a democracy only; and among others, the observation that it can never be established but among a small number of people, living within a small compass of territory.

Such a fallacy may have been the less perceived, as most of the popular governments of antiquity were of the democratic species; and even in modern Europe, to which we owe the great principle of representation, no example is seen of a government wholly popular, and founded, at the same time, wholly on that principle. If Europe has the merit of discovering this great mechanical power in government, by the simple agency of which the will of the largest political body may be concentered, and its force directed to any object which the public good requires, America can claim the merit of making the discovery the basis of unmixed and extensive republics. It is only to be lamented that any of her citizens should wish to deprive her of the additional merit of displaying its full efficacy in the establishment of the comprehensive system now under her consideration.

As the natural limit of a democracy is that distance from the central point which will just permit the most remote citizens to assemble as often as their public functions demand, and will include no greater number than can join in those functions, so the natural limit of a republic is that distance from the center which will barely allow the representatives of the people to meet as often as may be necessary for the administration of public affairs. Can it be said that the limits of the United States exceed this distance? It will not be said by those who recollect that the Atlantic coast is the longest side of the Union, that during the term of thirteen years the representatives of the states have been almost continually assembled, and that the members from the most distant states are not chargeable with greater intermissions of attendance than those from the states in the neighborhood of Congress.

That we may form a juster estimate with regard to this interesting subject, let us resort to the actual dimensions of the Union. The limits, as fixed by the treaty of peace, are: on the east the Atlantic, on the south the latitude of thirty-one degrees, on the west the Mississippi, and on the north an irregular line running in some instances beyond the forty-fifth degree, in others falling as low as the forty-second. The southern shore of Lake Erie lies below that latitude. Computing the distance between the thirty-first and forty-fifth degrees, it amounts to nine hundred and seventy-three common miles; computing it from thirty-one to forty-two degrees, to seven hundred, sixty-four miles and a half. Taking the mean for the distance, the amount will be eight hundred, sixty-eight miles and three fourths. The mean distance from the Atlantic to the Mississippi does not probably exceed seven hundred and fifty miles. On a comparison of this extent with that of several countries in Europe, the practicability of rendering our system commensurate to it appears to be demonstrable. It is not a great deal larger than Germany, where a diet representing the whole empire is continually assembled; or than Poland before the late dismemberment, where another national diet was the depositary of the supreme power. Passing by France and Spain, we find that in Great Britain, inferior as it may be in size, the representatives of the northern extremity of the island have as far to travel to the national council as will be required of those of the most remote parts of the Union.

Favorable as this view of the subject may be, some observations remain which will place it in a light still more satisfactory.

In the first place it is to be remembered that the general government is not to be charged with the whole power of making and administering laws. Its jurisdiction is limited to certain enumerated objects, which concern all the members of the republic, but which are not to be attained by the separate provisions of any. The subordinate governments, which can extend their care to all those other objects which can be separately provided for, will retain their due authority and activity. Were it proposed by the plan of the Convention to abolish the governments of the particular states, its adversaries would have some ground for their objection; though it would not be difficult to show that if they were abolished the general government would be compelled, by the principle of self-preservation, to reinstate them in their proper jurisdiction.

A second observation to be made is that the immediate object of the federal Constitution is to secure the union of the thirteen primitive states, which we know to be practicable; and to add to them such other states as may arise in their own bosoms, or in their neighborhoods, which we cannot doubt to be equally practicable. The arrangements that may be necessary for those angles and fractions of our territory which lie on our northwestern frontier, must be left to those whom further discoveries and experience will render more equal to the task.

Let it be remarked, in the third place, that the intercourse throughout the Union will be daily facilitated by new improvements. Roads will everywhere be shortened, and kept in better order; accommodations for travelers will be multiplied and meliorated; an interior navigation on our eastern side will be opened throughout, or nearly throughout, the whole extent of the thirteen states. The communication between the western and Atlantic districts, and between different parts of each, will be rendered more and more easy by those numerous canals with which the beneficence of nature has intersected our country, and which art finds it so little difficult to connect and complete.

A fourth and still more important consideration is, that as almost every state will, on one side or other, be a frontier, and will thus find, in a regard to its safety, an inducement to make some sacrifices for the sake of the general protection, so the states which lie at the greatest distance from the heart of the Union, and which, of course, may partake least of the ordinary circulation of its benefits, will be at the same time immediately contiguous to foreign nations, and will consequently stand, on particular occasions, in greatest need of its strength and resources. It may be inconvenient for Georgia, or the states forming our western or northeastern borders, to send their representatives to the seat of government; but they would find it more so to struggle alone against an invading enemy, or even to support alone the whole expense of those precautions which may be dictated by the neighborhood of continual danger. If they should derive less benefit, therefore, from the Union in some respects than the less distant states, they will derive greater benefit from it in other respects, and thus the proper equilibrium will be maintained throughout.

I submit to you, my fellow-citizens, these considerations, in full confidence that the good sense which has so often marked your decisions will allow them their due weight and effect; and that you will never suffer difficulties, however formidable in appearance, or however fashionable the error on which they may be founded, to drive you into the gloomy and perilous scenes into which the advocates for disunion would conduct you. Hearken not to the unnatural voice which tells you that the people of America, knit together as they are by so many cords of affection, can no longer live together as members of the same family, can no longer continue the mutual guardians of their mutual happiness, can no longer be fellow-citizens of one great, respectable, and flourishing empire. Hearken not to the voice which petulantly tells you that the form of government recommended for your adoption is a novelty in the political world; that it has never yet had a place in the theories of the wildest projectors; that it rashly attempts what it is impossible to accomplish. No, my countrymen, shut your ears against this unhallowed language. Shut your hearts against the poison which it conveys; the kindred blood which flows in the veins of American citizens, the mingled blood which they have shed in defense of their sacred rights, consecrate their Union, and excite horror at the idea of their becoming aliens, rivals, enemies. And if novelties are to be shunned, believe me, the most alarming of all novelties, the most wild of all projects, the most rash of all attempts, is that of rending us in pieces, in order to preserve our liberties and promote our happiness. But why is the experiment of an extended republic to be rejected, merely because it may comprise what is new? Is it not the glory of the people of America that, whilst they have paid a decent regard to the opinions of former times and other nations, they have not suffered a blind veneration for antiquity, for custom, or for names, to overrule the suggestions of their own good sense, the knowledge of their own situation, and the lessons of their own experience? To this manly spirit, posterity will be indebted for the possession, and the world for the example, of the numerous innovations displayed on the American theater, in favor of private rights and public happiness. Had no important step been taken by the leaders of the Revolution for which a precedent could not be discovered, no government established of which an exact model did not present itself, the people of the United States might, at this moment, have been numbered among the melancholy victims of misguided councils, must at best have been laboring under the weight of some of those forms which have crushed the liberties of the rest of mankind. Happily for America, happily, we trust, for the whole human race, they pursued a new and more noble course. They accomplished a revolution which has no parallel in the annals of human society. They reared the fabrics of governments which have no model on the face of the globe. They formed the design of a great confederacy, which it is incumbent on their successors to improve and perpetuate. If their works betray imperfections, we wonder at the fewness of them. If they erred most in the structure of the Union, this was the work most difficult to be executed; this is the work which has been new modeled by the act of your Convention, and it is that act on which you are now to deliberate and to decide.

PUBLIUS.

(b) THE LACK OF POWER TO COMPEL OBEDIENCE

FURTHER DEFECTS OF THE PRESENT CONSTITUTION [1]

Having in the three last numbers taken a summary review of the principal circumstances and events which depict the genius and fate of other confederate governments, I shall now proceed in the enumeration of the most important of those defects which have hitherto disappointed our hopes from the system established among ourselves. To form a safe and satisfactory judgment of the proper remedy, it is absolutely necessary that we should be well acquainted with the extent and malignity of the disease.

The next most palpable defect of the existing Confederation is the total want of a SANCTION to its laws. The United States, as now composed, have no power to exact obedience, or punish disobedience to their resolutions, either by pecuniary mulcts, by a suspension or divestiture of privileges, or by any other constitutional means. There is no express delegation of authority to them to use force against delinquent members; and if such a right should be ascribed to the federal head, as resulting from the nature of the social compact between the states, it must be by inference and construction, in the face of that part of the second article, by which it is declared, "that each state shall retain every power, jurisdiction, and right, not *expressly* delegated to the United States in Congress assembled." The want of such a right involves, no doubt, a striking absurdity; but we are reduced to the dilemma either of supposing that deficiency, preposterous as it may seem, or of contravening or explaining away a provision, which has been of late a repeated theme of the eulogies of those who oppose the new Constitution; and the omission of which, in that plan, has been the subject of much

[1] No. XXI. Hamilton. Independent Journal, December 12, 1787.

plausible animadversion and severe criticism. If we are unwilling to impair the force of this applauded provision, we shall be obliged to conclude that the United States afford the extraordinary spectacle of a government destitute even of the shadow of constitutional power to enforce the execution of its own laws. It will appear, from the specimens which have been cited, that the American Confederacy, in this particular, stands discriminated from every other institution of a similar kind, and exhibits a new and unexampled phenomenon in the political world.

The want of a mutual guarantee of the state governments is another capital imperfection in the federal plan. There is nothing of this kind declared in the articles that compose it; and to imply a tacit guarantee from considerations of utility, would be a still more flagrant departure from the clause which has been mentioned than to imply a tacit power of coercion from the like considerations. The want of a guarantee, though it might in its consequences endanger the Union, does not so immediately attack its existence as the want of a constitutional sanction to its laws.

Without a guarantee the assistance to be derived from the Union in repelling those domestic dangers which may sometimes threaten the existence of the state constitutions, must be renounced. Usurpation may rear its crest in each state, and trample upon the liberties of the people, while the national government could legally do nothing more than behold its encroachments with indignation and regret. A successful faction may erect a tyranny on the ruins of order and law, while no succor could constitutionally be afforded by the Union to the friends and supporters of the government. The tempestuous situation from which Massachusetts has scarcely emerged, evinces that dangers of this kind are not merely speculative. Who can determine what might have been the issue of her late convulsions, if the malcontents had been headed by a Cæsar or by a Cromwell? Who can predict what effect a despotism, established in Massachusetts, would have upon the liberties of New Hampshire or Rhode Island, of Connecticut or New York?

The inordinate pride of state importance has suggested to some minds an objection to the principle of a guarantee in the federal government, as involving an officious interference in the domestic concerns of the members. A scruple of this kind would deprive us of one of the principal advantages to be expected from union, and can only flow from a misapprehension of the nature of the provision itself. It could be no impediment to reforms of the state constitutions by a majority of the people in a legal and peaceable mode. This right would remain undiminished. The guarantee could only operate against changes to be effected by violence. Towards the prevention of calamities of this kind, too many checks cannot be provided. The peace of society and the stability of government depend absolutely on the efficacy of the precautions adopted on this head. Where the whole power of the government is in the hands of the people, there is the less pretence for the use of violent remedies in partial or occasional distempers of the state. The natural cure for an ill administration, in a popular or representative constitution, is a change of men. A guarantee by the national authority would be as much directed against the usurpations of rulers as against the ferments and outrages of faction and sedition in the community.

The principle of regulating the contributions of the states to the common treasury by QUOTAS is another fundamental error in the Confederation. Its repugnancy to an adequate supply of the national exigencies has been already pointed out, and has sufficiently appeared from the trial which has been made of it. I speak of it now solely with a view to equality among the states. Those who have been accustomed to contemplate the circumstances which produce and constitute national wealth, must be satisfied that there is no common standard or barometer by which the degrees of it can be ascertained. Neither the value of lands, nor the numbers of the people, which have been successively proposed as the rule of state contributions, has any pretension to being a just representative. If we compare the wealth of the United Netherlands with that of Russia or

Germany, or even of France, and if we at the same time compare the total value of the lands and the aggregate population of the contracted territory of that republic with the total value of the lands and the aggregate population of the immense regions of either of those kingdoms, we shall at once discover that there is no comparison between the proportion of either of these two objects and that of the relative wealth of those nations. If the like parallel were to be run between several of the American states, it would furnish a like result. Let Virginia be contrasted with North Carolina, Pennsylvania with Connecticut, or Maryland with New Jersey, and we shall be convinced that the respective abilities of those states, in relation to revenue, bear little or no analogy to their comparative stock in lands or to their comparative population. The position may be equally illustrated by a similar process between the counties of the same state. No man acquainted with the State of New York will doubt that the active wealth of King's County bears a much greater proportion to that of Montgomery than it would appear to do if we should take either the total value of the lands or the total numbers of the people as a criterion!

The wealth of nations depends upon an infinite variety of causes. Situation, soil, climate, the nature of the productions, the nature of the government, the genius of the citizens, the degree of information they possess, the state of commerce, of arts, of industry, — these circumstances and many more, too complex, minute, or adventitious to admit of a particular specification, occasion differences hardly conceivable in the relative opulence and riches of different countries. The consequence clearly is that there can be no common measure of national wealth, and, of course, no general or stationary rule by which the ability of a state to pay taxes can be determined. The attempt, therefore, to regulate the contributions of the members of a confederacy by any such rule, cannot fail to be productive of glaring inequality and extreme oppression.

This inequality would of itself be sufficient in America to work the eventual destruction of the Union, if any mode of enforcing a compliance with its requisitions could be devised. The suffering states would not long consent to remain associated upon a principle which distributed the public burdens with so unequal a hand, and which was calculated to impoverish and oppress the citizens of some states, while those of others would scarcely be conscious of the small proportion of the weight they were required to sustain. This, however, is an evil inseparable from the principle of quotas and requisitions.

There is no method of steering clear of this inconvenience, but by authorizing the national government to raise its own revenues in its own way. Imposts, excises, and, in general, all duties upon articles of consumption, may be compared to a fluid, which will, in time, find its level with the means of paying them. The amount to be contributed by each citizen will in a degree be at his own option, and can be regulated by an attention to his resources. The rich may be extravagant, the poor can be frugal; and private oppression may always be avoided by a judicious selection of objects proper for such impositions. If inequalities should arise in some states from duties on particular objects, these will, in all probability, be counterbalanced by proportional inequalities in other states, from the duties on other objects. In the course of time and things, an equilibrium, as far as it is attainable in so complicated a subject, will be established everywhere. Or, if inequalities should still exist, they would neither be so great in their degree, so uniform in their operation, nor so odious in their appearance, as those which would necessarily spring from quotas, upon any scale that can possibly be devised.

It is a signal advantage of taxes on articles of consumption that they contain in their own nature a security against excess. They prescribe their own limit, which cannot be exceeded without defeating the end proposed, — that is, an extension of the revenue. When applied to this object, the saying is as just as it is witty, that, " in political arithmetic, two and two do not always makes four." If duties are too high, they lessen the consumption, the collection is eluded, and the product to the treasury is not so great as when they are confined within proper and moderate bounds. This forms a complete barrier against any material oppression of the citizens by taxes of this class, and is itself a natural limitation of the power of imposing them.

Impositions of this kind usually fall under the denomination of indirect taxes, and must for a long time constitute the chief part of the revenue raised in this country. Those of the direct kind, which principally relate to lands and buildings, may admit of a rule of apportionment. Either the value of land, or the number of the people, may serve as a standard. The state of agriculture and the populousness of a country are considered as having a near relation to each other. And, as a rule, for the purpose intended, numbers, in the view of simplicity and certainty, are entitled to a preference. In every country it is an herculean task to obtain a valuation of the land; in a country imperfectly settled and progressive in improvement, the difficulties are increased almost to impracticability. The expense of an accurate valuation is, in all situations, a formidable objection. In a branch of taxation where no limits to the discretion of the government are to be found in the nature of the thing, the establishment of a fixed rule, not incompatible with the end, may be attended with fewer inconveniences than to leave that discretion altogether at large. PUBLIUS.

(c) THE LACK OF POWER TO REGULATE COMMERCE

THE SAME SUBJECT CONTINUED AND CONCLUDED [1]

In addition to the defects already enumerated in the existing federal system, there are others of not less importance, which concur in rendering it altogether unfit for the administration of the affairs of the Union.

The want of a power to regulate commerce is by all parties allowed to be of the number. The utility of such a power has been anticipated under the first head of our inquiries; and for this reason, as well as from the universal conviction entertained

[1] No. XXII. Hamilton. New York Packet, December 14, 1787.

upon the subject, little need be added in this place. It is indeed evident, on the most superficial view, that there is no object, either as it respects the interests of trade or finance, that more strongly demands a federal superintendence. The want of it has already operated as a bar to the formation of beneficial treaties with foreign powers, and has given occasions of dissatisfaction between the states. No nation acquainted with the nature of our political association would be unwise enough to enter into stipulations with the United States, conceding on their part privileges of importance, while they were apprised that the engagements on the part of the Union might at any moment be violated by its members, and while they found from experience that they might enjoy every advantage they desired in our markets, without granting us any return but such as their momentary convenience might suggest. It is not, therefore, to be wondered at that Mr. Jenkinson, in ushering into the House of Commons a bill for regulating the temporary intercourse between the two countries, should preface its introduction by a declaration that similar provisions in former bills had been found to answer every purpose to the commerce of Great Britain, and that it would be prudent to persist in the plan until it should appear whether the American government was likely or not to acquire greater consistency.[1]

Several states have endeavored, by separate prohibitions, restrictions, and exclusions, to influence the conduct of that kingdom in this particular, but the want of concert, arising from the want of a general authority and from clashing and dissimilar views in the states, has hitherto frustrated every experiment of the kind, and will continue to do so as long as the same obstacles to an uniformity of measures continue to exist.

The interfering and unneighborly regulations of some states, contrary to the true spirit of the Union, have, in different instances, given just cause of umbrage and complaint to others, and it is to be feared that examples of this nature, if not re-

[1] This, as nearly as I can recollect, was the sense of this speech in introducing the last bill.

strained by a national control, would be multiplied and extended till they became not less serious sources of animosity and discord than injurious impediments to the intercourse between the different parts of the Confederacy. "The commerce of the German empire[1] is in continual trammels from the multiplicity of the duties which the several princes and states exact upon the merchandises passing through their territories, by means of which the fine streams and navigable rivers with which Germany is so happily watered are rendered almost useless." Though the genius of the people of this country might never permit this description to be strictly applicable to us, yet we may reasonably expect, from the gradual conflicts of state regulations, that the citizens of each would at length come to be considered and treated by the others in no better light than that of foreigners and aliens.

The power of raising armies, by the most obvious construction of the Articles of the Confederation, is merely a power of making requisitions upon the states for quotas of men. This practice, in the course of the late war, was found replete with obstructions to a vigorous and to an economical system of defense. It gave birth to a competition between the states which created a kind of auction for men. In order to furnish the quotas required of them, they outbid each other till bounties grew to an enormous and insupportable size. The hope of a still further increase afforded an inducement to those who were disposed to serve to procrastinate their enlistment, and disinclined them to engage for any considerable periods. Hence, slow and scanty levies of men, in the most critical emergencies of our affairs; short enlistments at an unparalleled expense; continual fluctuations in the troops, ruinous to their discipline and subjecting the public safety frequently to the perilous crisis of a disbanded army. Hence, also, those oppressive expedients for raising men which were upon several occasions practiced, and which nothing but the enthusiasm of liberty would have induced the people to endure.

[1] Encyclopaedia, article "Empire."

This method of raising troops is not more unfriendly to economy and vigor than it is to an equal distribution of the burden. The states near the seat of war, influenced by motives of self-preservation, made efforts to furnish their quotas, which even exceeded their abilities, while those at a distance from danger were, for the most part, as remiss as the others were diligent, in their exertions. The immediate pressure of this inequality was not in this case, as in that of the contributions of money, alleviated by the hope of a final liquidation. The states which did not pay their proportions of money might at least be charged with their deficiencies; but no account could be formed of the deficiencies in the supplies of men. We shall not, however, see much reason to regret the want of this hope, when we consider how little prospect there is that the most delinquent states ever will be able to make compensation for their pecuniary failures. The system of quotas and requisitions, whether it be applied to men or money, is, in every view, a system of imbecility in the Union, and of inequality and injustice among the members.

The right of equal suffrage among the states is another exceptionable part of the Confederation. Every idea of proportion and every rule of fair representation conspire to condemn a principle which gives to Rhode Island an equal weight in the scale of power with Massachusetts, or Connecticut, or New York, and to Delaware an equal voice in the national deliberations with Pennsylvania, or Virginia, or North Carolina. Its operation contradicts that fundamental maxim of republican government, which requires that the sense of the majority should prevail. Sophistry may reply that sovereigns are equal, and that a majority of the votes of the states will be a majority of confederated America. But this kind of logical legerdemain will never counteract the plain suggestions of justice and common sense. It may happen that this majority of states is a small minority of the people of America;[1] and two thirds of the

[1] New Hampshire, Rhode Island, New Jersey, Delaware, Georgia, South Carolina, and Maryland are a majority of the whole number of the states, but they do not contain one third of the people.

people of America could not long be persuaded, upon the credit of artificial distinctions and syllogistic subtleties, to submit their interests to the management and disposal of one third. The larger states would after a while revolt from the idea of receiving the law from the smaller. To acquiesce in such a privation of their due importance in the political scale, would be not merely to be insensible to the love of power, but even to sacrifice the desire of equality. It is neither rational to expect the first, nor just to require the last. The smaller states, considering how peculiarly their safety and welfare depend on union, ought readily to renounce a pretension which, if not relinquished, would prove fatal to its duration.

It may be objected to this, that not seven but nine states, or two thirds of the whole number, must consent to the most important resolutions; and it may be thence inferred that nine states would always comprehend a majority of the inhabitants of the Union. But this does not obviate the impropriety of an equal vote between states of the most unequal dimensions and populousness; nor is the inference accurate in point of fact, for we can enumerate nine states which contain less than a majority of the people,[2] and it is constitutionally possible that these nine may give the vote. Besides, there are matters of considerable moment determinable by a bare majority; and there are others, concerning which doubts have been entertained, which, if interpreted in favor of the sufficiency of a vote of seven states, would extend its operation to interests of the first magnitude. In addition to this, it is to be observed that there is a probability of an increase in the number of states, and no provision for a proportional augmentation of the ratio of votes.

But this is not all: what at first sight may seem a remedy, is, in reality, a poison. To give a minority a negative upon the majority (which is always the case where more than a majority is requisite to a decision), is, in its tendency, to subject the sense of the greater number to that of the lesser. Congress, from the

[2] Add New York and Connecticut to the foregoing seven, and they will still be less than a majority.

non-attendance of a few states, have been frequently in the situation of a Polish diet, where a single VETO has been sufficient to put a stop to all their movements. A sixtieth part of the Union, which is about the proportion of Delaware and Rhode Island, has several times been able to oppose an entire bar to its operations. This is one of those refinements which, in practice, has an effect the reverse of what is expected from it in theory. The necessity of unanimity in public bodies, or of something approaching towards it, has been founded upon a supposition that it would contribute to security. But its real operation is to embarrass the administration, to destroy the energy of government, and to substitute the pleasure, caprice, or artifices of an insignificant, turbulent, or corrupt junto, to the regular deliberations and decisions of a respectable majority. In those emergencies of a nation, in which the goodness or badness, the weakness or strength of its government, is of the greatest importance, there is commonly a necessity for action. The public business must, in some way or other, go forward. If a pertinacious minority can control the opinion of a majority respecting the best mode of conducting it, the majority, in order that something may be done, must conform to the views of the minority; and thus the sense of the smaller number will overrule that of the greater, and give a tone to the national proceedings. Hence, tedious delays, continual negotiation and intrigue, contemtemptible compromises of the public good. And yet, in such a system, it is even happy when such compromises can take place; for upon some occasions things will not admit of accommodation, and then the measures of government must be injuriously suspended, or fatally defeated. It is often, by the impracticability of obtaining the concurrence of the necessary number of votes, kept in a state of inaction. Its situation must always savor of weakness, sometimes border upon anarchy.

It is not difficult to discover that a principle of this kind gives greater scope to foreign corruption, as well as to domestic faction, than that which permits the sense of the majority to decide, though the contrary of this has been presumed. The mistake has proceeded from not attending with due care to the mischiefs that may be occasioned by obstructing the progress of government at certain critical seasons. When the concurrence of a large number is required by the Constitution to the doing of any national act, we are apt to rest satisfied that all is safe, because nothing improper will be likely *to be done;* but we forget how much good may be prevented, and how much ill may be produced, by the power of hindering that which is necessary from being done, and of keeping affairs in the same unfavorable posture in which they may happen to stand at particular periods.

Suppose, for instance, we were engaged in a war, in conjunction with one foreign nation, against another. Suppose the necessity of our situation demanded peace, and the interest or ambition of our ally led him to seek the prosecution of the war, with views that might justify us in making separate terms. In such a state of things, this ally of ours would evidently find it much easier, by his bribes and his intrigues, to tie up the hands of government from making peace, where two thirds of all the votes were requisite to that object, than where a simple majority would suffice. In the first case, he would have to corrupt a smaller number; in the last, a greater number. Upon the same principle, it would be much easier for a foreign power with which we were at war to perplex our councils and embarrass our exertions. And, in a commercial view, we may be subjected to similar inconveniences. A nation, with which we might have a treaty of commerce, could with much greater facility prevent our forming a connection with her competitor in trade, though such a connection should be ever so beneficial to ourselves.

Evils of this description ought not to be regarded as imaginary. One of the weak sides of republics, among their numerous advantages, is that they afford too easy an inlet to foreign corruption. An hereditary monarch, though often disposed to sacrifice his subjects to his ambition, has so great a personal interest in the government and in the external glory of the nation, that it is not easy for a foreign power to give him an equivalent for what he would sacrifice by treachery to the state. The world has accordingly been witness to few examples of this species of royal prostitution, though there have been abundant specimens of every other kind.

In republics, persons elevated from the mass of the community, by the suffrages of their fellow-citizens, to stations of great preëminence and power, may find compensations for betraying their trust, which, to any but minds actuated by superior virtue, may appear to exceed the proportion of interest they have in the common stock, and to overbalance the obligations of duty. Hence it is that history furnishes us with so many mortifying examples of the prevalency of foreign corruption in republican governments. How much this contributed to the ruin of the ancient commonwealths has been already disclosed. It is well known that the deputies of the United Provinces have, in various instances, been purchased by the emissaries of the neighboring kingdoms. The Earl of Chesterfield (if my memory serves me right), in a letter to his court, intimates that his success in an important negotiation must depend on his obtaining a major's commission for one of those deputies. And in Sweden the parties were alternately bought by France and England in so barefaced and notorious a manner that it excited universal disgust in the nation, and was a principal cause that the most limited monarch in Europe, in a single day, without tumult, violence, or opposition, became one of the most absolute and uncontrolled.

A circumstance which crowns the defects of the Confederation remains yet to be mentioned — the want of a judiciary power. Laws are a dead letter without courts to expound and define their true meaning and operation. The treaties of the United States, to have any force at all, must be considered as part of the law of the land. Their true import, as far as respects individuals, must, like all other laws, be ascertained by judicial determinations. To produce uniformity in these determinations, they ought to be submitted, in the last resort, to one SUPREME TRIBUNAL. And this tribunal ought to be instituted under the same authority which forms the treaties themselves. These ingredients are both indispensable. If there is in each state a court of final jurisdiction, there may be as many different final determinations on the same point as there are courts. There are endless diversities in the opinions of men. We often see not only different courts but the judges of the same court differing from each other. To avoid the confusion which would unavoidably result from the contradictory decisions of a number of independent judicatories, all nations have found it necessary to establish one court paramount to the rest, possessing a general superintendence, and authorized to settle and declare in the last resort an uniform rule of civil justice.

This is the more necessary where the frame of the government is so compounded that the laws of the whole are in danger of being contravened by the laws of the parts. In this case, if the particular tribunals are invested with a right of ultimate jurisdiction, besides the contradictions to be expected from difference of opinion, there will be much to fear from the bias of local views and prejudices, and from the interference of local regulations. As often as such an interference was to happen, there would be reason to apprehend that the provisions of the particular laws might be preferred to those of the general laws, from the deference with which men in office naturally look up to that authority to which they owe their official existence. The treaties of the United States, under the present Constitution, are liable to the infractions of thirteen different legislatures, and as many different courts of final jurisdiction, acting under the authority of those legislatures. The faith, the reputation, the peace of the whole Union, are thus continually at the mercy of the prejudices, the passions, and the interests of every member of which it is composed. Is it possible that foreign nations can either respect or confide in such a government? Is it possible that the people of America will longer consent to trust their honor, their happiness, their safety, on so precarious a foundation?

In this review of the Confederation, I have confined myself to the exhibition of its most material defects, passing over those imperfections in its details by which even a considerable part of the power intended to be conferred upon it has been in a great measure rendered abortive. It must be by this time evident to all men of reflection who are either free from erroneous prepossessions or can divest themselves of them, that it is a system so radically vicious and unsound as to admit not of amendment but by an entire change in its leading features and characters.

The organization of Congress is itself utterly improper for the exercise of those powers which are necessary to be deposited in the Union. A single assembly may be a proper receptacle of those slender, or rather fettered, authorities, which have been heretofore delegated to the federal head; but it would be inconsistent with all the principles of good government to intrust it with those additional powers which, even the moderate and more rational adversaries of the proposed Constitution admit, ought to reside in the United States. If that plan should not be adopted, and if the necessity of union should be able to withstand the ambitious aims of those men who may indulge magnificent schemes of personal aggrandizement from its dissolution, the probability would be that we should run into the project of conferring supplementary powers upon Congress, as they are now constituted; and either the machine, from the intrinsic feebleness of its structure, will moulder into pieces, in spite of our ill-judged efforts to prop it, or, by successive augmentations of its force and energy, as necessity might prompt, we shall finally accumulate, in a single body, all the most important prerogatives of sovereignty, and thus entail upon our posterity one of the most execrable forms of government that human infatuation ever contrived. Thus we should create in reality that very tyranny which the adversaries of the new Constitution either are, or affect to be, solicitous to avert.

It has not a little contributed to the infirmities of the existing federal system, that it never had a ratification by the PEOPLE. Resting on no better foundation than the consent of the several legislatures, it has been exposed to frequent and intricate questions concerning the validity of its powers, and has, in some instances, given birth to the enormous doctrine of a right of legislative repeal. Owing its ratification to the law of a state, it has been contended that the same authority might repeal the law by which it was ratified. However gross a heresy it may be to maintain that a *party* to a *compact* has a right to revoke that *compact*, the doctrine itself has had respectable advocates. The possibility of a question of this nature proves the necessity of laying the foundations of our national government deeper than in the mere sanction of delegated authority. The fabric of American empire ought to rest on the solid basis of THE CONSENT OF THE PEOPLE. The streams of national power ought to flow immediately from that pure, original fountain of all legitimate authority.

PUBLIUS.

IV

DIFFICULTIES ENCOUNTERED IN FRAMING THE NEW CONSTITUTION

(a) INHERENT DIFFICULTIES OF THE UNDERTAKING

Concerning the Difficulties which the Convention must have experienced in the Formulation of a proper Plan [1]

In reviewing the defects of the existing Confederation, and showing that they cannot be supplied by a government of less energy than that before the public, several of the most important principles of the latter fell of course under consideration. But as the ultimate object of these papers is to determine clearly and fully the merits of this Constitution, and the expediency of adopting it, our plan cannot be completed without taking a more critical and thorough survey of the work of the Convention, without examining it on all its sides, comparing it in all its parts, and calculating its probable effects.

That this remaining task may be executed under impressions conducive to a just and fair result, some reflections must in this place be indulged, which candor previously suggests.

It is a misfortune, inseparable from human affairs, that public measures are rarely investigated with that spirit of moderation which is essential to a just estimate of their real tendency to advance or obstruct the public good; and that this spirit is more apt to be diminished than promoted by those occasions which require an unusual exercise of it. To those who have been led by experience to attend to this consideration, it could not appear surprising that the act of the Convention, which recommends so many important changes and innovations, which may be viewed in so many lights and relations, and which touches the springs of so many passions and interests, should

[1] No. XXXVII (XXXVI). Madison. Daily Advertiser, January 11, 1788.

find or excite dispositions unfriendly, both on one side and on the other, to a fair discussion and accurate judgment of its merits. In some, it has been too evident from their own publications that they have scanned the proposed Constitution, not only with a predisposition to censure, but with a predetermination to condemn; as the language held by others betrays an opposite predetermination or bias, which must render their opinions also of little moment in the question. In placing, however, these different characters on a level, with respect to the weight of their opinions, I wish not to insinuate that there may not be a material difference in the purity of their intentions. It is but just to remark in favor of the latter description, that as our situation is universally admitted to be peculiarly critical, and to require indispensably that something should be done for our relief, the predetermined patron of what has been actually done may have taken his bias from the weight of these considerations, as well as from considerations of a sinister nature. The predetermined adversary, on the other hand, can have been governed by no venial motive whatever. The intentions of the first may be upright, as they may on the contrary be culpable. The views of the last cannot be upright, and must be culpable. But the truth is, that these papers are not addressed to persons falling under either of these characters. They solicit the attention of those only who add to a sincere zeal for the happiness of their country a temper favorable to a just estimate of the means of promoting it.

Persons of this character will proceed to an examination of the plan submitted by the Convention, not only without a disposition to find or to magnify faults, but will see the propriety of reflecting that a faultless plan was not to be expected. Nor will they barely make allowances for the errors which may be chargeable on the fallibility to which the Convention, as a body of men, were liable; but will keep in mind that they themselves also are but men, and ought not to assume an infallibility in rejudging the fallible opinions of others.

With equal readiness will it be perceived that, besides these inducements to candor, many allowances ought to be made for the difficulties inherent in the very nature of the undertaking referred to the Convention.

The novelty of the undertaking immediately strikes us. It has been shown in the course of these papers, that the existing Confederation is founded on principles which are fallacious; that we must consequently change this first foundation, and with it the superstructure resting upon it. It has been shown that the other confederacies which could be consulted as precedents have been vitiated by the same erroneous principles, and can therefore furnish no other light than that of beacons which give warning of the course to be shunned, without pointing out that which ought to be pursued. The most that the Convention could do in such a situation was to avoid the errors suggested by the past experience of other countries, as well as of our own, and to provide a convenient mode of rectifying their own errors, as future experience may unfold them.

Among the difficulties encountered by the Convention, a very important one must have lain in combining the requisite stability and energy in government with the inviolable attention due to liberty and to the republican form. Without substantially accomplishing this part of their undertaking, they would have very imperfectly fulfilled the object of their appointment, or the expectation of the public; yet that it could not be easily accomplished will be denied by no one who is unwilling to betray his ignorance of the subject. Energy in government is essential to that security against external and internal danger, and to that prompt and salutary execution of the laws which enter into the very definition of good government. Stability in government is essential to national character and to the advantages annexed to it, as well as to that repose and confidence in the minds of the people, which are among the chief blessings of civil society. An irregular and mutable legislation is not more an evil in itself than it is odious to the people; and it may be pronounced with assurance that the people of this country, enlightened as they are with regard to the nature, and interested, as the great body of them are, in the effects of good government, will never be satisfied till some remedy be applied to the vicissitudes and uncertainties which characterize the state administrations. On comparing, however, these valuable ingredients with the vital principles of liberty, we must perceive at once the difficulty of mingling them together in their due proportions. The genius of republican liberty seems to demand on one side not only that all power should be derived from the people, but that those intrusted with it should be kept in dependence on the people, by a short duration of their appointments; and that even during this short period the trust should be placed not in a few, but in a number of hands. Stability, on the contrary, requires that the hands in which power is lodged should continue for a length of time the same. A frequent change of men will result from a frequent return of elections, and a frequent change of measures from a frequent change of men; whilst energy in government requires not only a certain duration of power, but the execution of it by a single hand.

How far the Convention may have succeeded in this part of their work, will better appear on a more accurate view of it. From the cursory view here taken, it must clearly appear to have been an arduous part.

Not less arduous must have been the task of marking the proper line of partition between the authority of the general and that of the state governments. Every man will be sensible of this difficulty, in proportion as he has been accustomed to contemplate and discriminate objects extensive and complicated in their nature. The faculties of the mind itself have never yet been distinguished and defined, with satisfactory precision, by all the efforts of the most acute and metaphysical philosophers. Sense, perception, judgment, desire, volition, memory, imagination, are found to be separated by such delicate shades and minute gradations that their boundaries have eluded the most subtle investigations, and remain a pregnant source of ingenious disquisition and controversy. The boundaries between the great kingdoms of nature, and, still more, between the various provinces and lesser portions into which they are subdivided, afford another illustration of the same important truth. The most sagacious and laborious naturalists have never yet succeeded in tracing with certainty the line which separates the district of vegetable life from the neighboring region of unorganized matter, or which marks the termination of the former and the commencement of the animal empire. A still greater obscurity lies in the distinctive characters by which the objects in each of these great departments of nature have been arranged and assorted.

When we pass from the works of nature, in which all the delineations are perfectly accurate, and appear to be otherwise only from the imperfection of the eye which surveys them, to the institutions of man, in which the obscurity arises as well from the object itself as from the organ by which it is contemplated, we must perceive the necessity of moderating still further our expectations and hopes from the efforts of human sagacity. Experience has instructed us that no skill in the science of government has yet been able to discriminate and define, with sufficient certainty, its three great provinces — the legislative, executive, and judiciary; or even the privileges and powers of the different legislative branches. Questions daily occur in the course of practice which prove the obscurity which reigns in these subjects, and which puzzle the greatest adepts in political science.

The experience of ages, with the continued and combined labors of the most enlightened legislators and jurists, have been equally unsuccessful in delineating the several objects and limits of different codes of laws and different tribunals of justice. The precise extent of the common law, the statute law, the maritime law, the ecclesiastical law, the law of corporations, and other local laws and customs, remains still to be clearly and finally established in Great Britain, where accuracy in such subjects has been more industriously pursued than in any other part of the world. The jurisdiction of her several courts, general and local, of law, of equity, of admiralty, etc., is not less a source of frequent and intricate discussions, sufficiently denoting the indeterminate limits by which they are respectively circumscribed. All new laws, though penned with the greatest technical skill, and passed on the fullest and most mature deliberation, are considered as more or less obscure and equivocal, until their meaning be liquidated and ascertained by a series of particular discussions and adjudications. Besides the obscurity arising from the complexity of objects, and the imperfection of the human faculties, the medium through which the conceptions of men are conveyed to each other adds a fresh embarrassment. The use of words is to express ideas. Perspicuity, therefore, requires not only that the ideas should be distinctly formed, but that they should be expressed by words distinctly and exclusively appropriated to them. But no language is so copious as to supply words and phrases for every complex idea, or so correct as not to include many equivocally denoting different ideas. Hence it must happen that however accurately objects may be discriminated in themselves, and however accurately the discrimination may be considered, the definition of them may be rendered inaccurate by the inaccuracy of the terms in which it is delivered. And this unavoidable inaccuracy must be greater or less, according to the complexity and novelty of the objects defined. When the Almighty himself condescends to address mankind in their own language, his meaning, luminous as it must be, is rendered dim and doubtful by the cloudy medium through which it is communicated.

Here, then, are three sources of vague and incorrect definitions: indistinctness of the object, imperfection of the organ of conception, inadequateness of the vehicle of ideas. Any one of these must produce a certain degree of obscurity. The Convention, in delineating the boundary between the federal and state jurisdictions, must have experienced the full effect of them all.

To the difficulties already mentioned may be added the interfering pretensions of the larger and smaller states. We cannot err in supposing that the former would contend for a participation in the government, fully proportioned to their superior wealth and importance; and that the latter would not be less tenacious of the equality at present enjoyed by them. We may well suppose that neither side would entirely yield to the other, and consequently that the struggle could be terminated only by compromise. It is extremely probable, also, that after the ratio of representation had been adjusted, this very compromise must have produced a fresh struggle between the same parties, to give such a turn to the organization of the government, and to the distribution of its powers, as would increase the importance of the branches, in forming which they had respectively obtained the greatest share of influence. There are features in the Constitution which warrant each of these suppositions; and as far as either of them is well founded, it shows that the Convention must have been compelled to sacrifice theoretical propriety to the force of extraneous considerations.

Nor could it have been the large and small states only, which would marshal themselves in opposition to each other on various points. Other combinations, resulting from a difference of local position and policy, must have created additional difficulties. As every state may be divided into different districts, and its citizens into different classes, which give birth to contending interests and local jealousies, so the different parts of the United States are distinguished from each other by a variety of circumstances which produce a like effect on a larger scale. And although this variety of interests, for reasons sufficiently explained in a former paper, may have a salutary influence on the administration of the government when formed, yet every one must be sensible of the contrary influence which must have been experienced in the task of forming it.

Would it be wonderful if, under the pressure of all these difficulties, the Convention should have been forced into some deviations from that artificial structure and regular symmetry which an abstract view of the subject might lead an ingenious theorist to bestow on a Constitution planned in his closet or in his imagination ? The real wonder is that so many difficulties should have been surmounted, and surmounted with an unanimity almost as unprecedented as it must have been unexpected. It is impossible for any man of candor to reflect on this circumstance without partaking of the astonishment. It is impossible for the man of pious reflection not to perceive in it a finger of that Almighty Hand which has been so frequently and signally extended to our relief in the critical stages of the Revolution.

We had occasion, in a former paper, to take notice of the repeated trials which have been unsuccessfully made in the United Netherlands for reforming the baneful and notorious vices of their constitution. The history of almost all the great councils and consultations held among mankind for reconciling their discordant opinions, assuaging their mutual jealousies, and adjusting their respective interests, is a history of factions, contentions, and disappointments, and may be classed among the most dark and degrading pictures which display the infirmities and depravities of the human character. If, in a few scattered instances, a brighter aspect is presented, they serve only as exceptions to admonish us of the general truth, and by their luster to darken the gloom of the adverse prospect to which they are contrasted. In revolving the causes from which these exceptions result, and applying them to the particular instance before us, we are necessarily led to two important conclusions. The first is, that the Convention must have enjoyed, in a very singular degree, an exemption from the pestilential influence of party animosities — the diseases most incident to deliberative bodies, and most apt to contaminate their proceedings. The second conclusion is that all the deputations composing the Convention were either satisfactorily accommodated by the final act, or were induced to accede to it by a deep conviction of the necessity of sacrificing private opinions and partial interests to the public good, and by a despair of seeing this necessity diminished by delays or by new experiments.

PUBLIUS.

(b) DIFFERENCE OF OPINION CONCERNING DETAILS

THE SUBJECT CONTINUED, AND THE INCOHERENCE OF THE OBJECTIONS TO THE PLAN EXPOSED[1]

It is not a little remarkable that in every case reported by ancient history, in which government has been established with deliberation and consent, the task of framing it has not been committed to an assembly of men, but has been performed by some individual citizen of preëminent wisdom and approved integrity.

Minos, we learn, was the primitive founder of the government of Crete, as Zaleucus was of that of the Locrians. Theseus first, and after him Draco and Solon, instituted the government of Athens. Lycurgus was the lawgiver of Sparta. The foundation of the original government of Rome was laid by Romulus, and the work completed by two of his elective successors, Numa and Tullus Hostilius. On the abolition of royalty the consular administration was substituted by Brutus, who stepped forward with a project for such a reform, which, he alleged, had been prepared by Servius Tullius, and to which his address obtained the assent and ratification of the senate and people. This remark is applicable to confederate governments also. Amphictyon, we are told, was the author of that which bore his name. The Achæan League received its first birth from Achæus, and its second from Aratus.

What degree of agency these reputed lawgivers might have in their respective establishments, or how far they might be clothed with the legitimate authority of the people, cannot in every instance be ascertained. In some, however, the proceeding was strictly regular. Draco appears to have been intrusted by the people of Athens with indefinite powers to reform its government and laws. And Solon, according to Plutarch, was in a manner compelled, by the universal suffrage of his fellow-citizens, to take upon him the sole and absolute power of new-modeling the constitution. The proceedings under Lycurgus

[1] No. XXXVIII (XXXVII). Madison. Independent Journal, January 12, 1788.

were less regular; but as far as the advocates for a regular reform could prevail, they all turned their eyes towards the single efforts of that celebrated patriot and sage, instead of seeking to bring about a revolution by the intervention of a deliberative body of citizens.

Whence could it have proceeded that a people, jealous as the Greeks were of their liberty, should so far abandon the rules of caution as to place their destiny in the hands of a single citizen? Whence could it have proceeded that the Athenians, a people who would not suffer an army to be commanded by fewer than ten generals, and who required no other proof of danger to their liberties than the illustrious merit of a fellow-citizen, should consider one illustrious citizen as a more eligible depositary of the fortunes of themselves and their posterity than a select body of citizens from whose common deliberations more wisdom, as well as more safety, might have been expected? These questions cannot be fully answered without supposing that the fears of discord and disunion among a number of counselors exceeded the apprehension of treachery or incapacity in a single individual. History informs us, likewise, of the difficulties with which these celebrated reformers had to contend, as well as of the expedients which they were obliged to employ in order to carry their reforms into effect. Solon, who seems to have indulged a more temporizing policy, confessed that he had not given to his countrymen the government best suited to their happiness, but most tolerable to their prejudices. And Lycurgus, more true to his object, was under the necessity of mixing a portion of violence with the authority of superstition, and of securing his final success by a voluntary renunciation, first of his country, and then of his life. If these lessons teach us, on one hand, to admire the improvement made by America on the ancient mode of preparing and establishing regular plans of government, they serve not less, on the other, to admonish us of the hazards and difficulties incident to such experiments, and of the great imprudence of unnecessarily multiplying them.

Is it an unreasonable conjecture that the errors which may

be contained in the plan of the Convention are such as have resulted rather from the defect of antecedent experience on this complicated and difficult subject, than from a want of accuracy or care in the investigation of it; and consequently, such, as will not be ascertained until an actual trial shall have pointed them out? This conjecture is rendered probable, not only by many considerations of a general nature, but by the particular case of the Articles of Confederation. It is observable that among the numerous objections and amendments suggested by the several states, when these articles were submitted for their ratification, not one is found which alludes to the great and radical error which on actual trial has discovered itself. And if we except the observations which New Jersey was led to make, rather by her local situation than by her peculiar foresight, it may be questioned whether a single suggestion was of sufficient moment to justify a revision of the system. There is abundant reason, nevertheless, to suppose that immaterial as these objections were, they would have been adhered to with a very dangerous inflexibility, in some states, had not a zeal for their opinions and supposed interests been stifled by the more powerful sentiment of self-preservation. One state, we may remember, persisted for several years in refusing her concurrence, although the enemy remained the whole period at our gates, or rather in the very bowels of our country. Nor was her pliancy in the end effected by a less motive than the fear of being chargeable with protracting the public calamities, and endangering the event of the contest. Every candid reader will make the proper reflections on these important facts.

A patient who finds his disorder daily growing worse, and that an efficacious remedy can no longer be delayed without extreme danger, after coolly revolving his situation, and the characters of different physicians, selects and calls in such of them as he judges most capable of administering relief, and best entitled to his confidence. The physicians attend; the case of the patient is carefully examined; a consultation is held; they are unanimously agreed that the symptoms are critical, but that the case, with proper and timely relief, is so far from being desperate that it may be made to issue in an improvement of his constitution. They are equally unanimous in prescribing the remedy by which this happy effect is to be produced. The prescription is no sooner made known, however, than a number of persons interpose, and, without denying the reality or danger of the disorder, assure the patient that the prescription will be poison to his constitution, and forbid him, under pain of certain death, to make use of it. Might not the patient reasonably demand, before he ventured to follow this advice, that the authors of it should at least agree among themselves on some other remedy to be substituted? And if he found them differing as much from one another as from his first counselors, would he not act prudently in trying the experiment unanimously recommended by the latter, rather than in hearkening to those who could neither deny the necessity of a speedy remedy, nor agree in proposing one?

Such a patient and in such a situation is America at this moment. She has been sensible of her malady. She has obtained a regular and unanimous advice from men of her own deliberate choice. And she is warned by others against following this advice under pain of the most fatal consequences. Do the monitors deny the reality of her danger? No. Do they deny the necessity of some speedy and powerful remedy? No. Are they agreed, are any two of them agreed, in their objections to the remedy proposed, or in the proper one to be substituted? Let them speak for themselves. This one tells us that the proposed Constitution ought to be rejected, because it is not a confederation of the states, but a government over individuals. Another admits that it ought to be a government over individuals, to a certain extent, but by no means to the extent proposed. A third does not object to the government over individuals, or to the extent proposed, but to the want of a bill of rights. A fourth concurs in the absolute necessity of a bill of rights, but contends that it ought to be declaratory, not of the personal rights of individuals, but of the rights reserved to the states in their political capacity. A fifth is of opinion that a bill of rights of any sort would be superfluous and misplaced, and that the plan would be unexceptionable but for the fatal power of regulating the times and places of election. An objector in a large state exclaims loudly against the unreasonable equality of representation in the Senate. An objector in a small state is equally loud against the dangerous inequality in the House of Representatives. From this quarter, we are alarmed with the amazing expense from the number of persons who are to administer the new government. From another quarter, and sometimes from the same quarter, on another occasion, the cry is that the Congress will be but the shadow of a representation, and that the government would be far less objectionable if the number and the expense were doubled. A patriot in a state that does not import or export discerns insuperable objections against the power of direct taxation. The patriotic adversary in a state of great exports and imports is not less dissatisfied that the whole burden of taxes may be thrown on consumption. This politician discovers in the Constitution a direct and irresistible tendency to monarchy; that is equally sure it will end in aristocracy. Another is puzzled to say which of these shapes it will ultimately assume, but sees clearly it must be one or other of them; whilst a fourth is not wanting, who with no less confidence affirms that the Constitution is so far from having a bias towards either of these dangers that the weight on that side will not be sufficient to keep it upright and firm against its opposite propensities. With another class of adversaries to the Constitution the language is that the legislative, executive, and judiciary departments are intermixed in such a manner as to contradict all the ideas of regular government and all the requisite precautions in favor of liberty. Whilst this objection circulates in vague and general expressions, there are not a few who lend their sanction to it. Let each one come forward with his particular explanation, and scarce any two are exactly agreed on the subject. In the eyes of one the junction of the Senate with the President in the responsible function of appointing to offices, instead of vesting this executive power in the executive alone, is the vicious part of the organization. To another, the exclusion of the House of Representatives, whose numbers alone could be a due security against corruption and partiality in the exercise of such a power, is equally obnoxious. With another, the admission of the President into any share of a power which must ever be a dangerous engine in the hands of the executive magistrate, is an unpardonable violation of the maxims of republican jealousy. No part of the arrangement, according to some, is more admissible than the trial of impeachments by the Senate, which is alternately a member both of the legislative and executive departments, when this power so evidently belonged to the judiciary department. We concur fully, reply others, in the objection to this part of the plan, but we can never agree that a reference of impeachments to the judiciary authority would be an amendment of the error. Our principal dislike to the organization arises from the extensive powers already lodged in that department. Even among the zealous patrons of a council of state the most irreconcilable variance is discovered concerning the mode in which it ought to be constituted. The demand of one gentleman is that the council should consist of a small number to be appointed by the most numerous branch of the legislature. Another would prefer a larger number, and considers it as a fundamental condition that the appointment should be made by the President himself.

As it can give no umbrage to the writers against the plan of the federal Constitution, let us suppose that as they are the most zealous, so they are also the most sagacious of those who think the late Convention were unequal to the task assigned them, and that a wiser and better plan might and ought to be substituted. Let us further suppose that their country should concur, both in this favorable opinion of their merits, and in their unfavorable opinion of the Convention; and should accordingly proceed to form them into a second convention, with full powers, and for the express purpose of revising and remolding the work of the first. Were the experiment to be seriously made, though it requires some effort to view it seriously even in fiction, I leave it to be decided by the sample of opinions just exhibited, whether, with all their enmity to their predecessors, they would, in any one point, depart so widely from their example, as in the discord and ferment that would mark their own deliberations; and whether the Constitution now before the public would not stand as fair a chance for immortality as Lycurgus gave to that of Sparta, by making its change to depend on his own return from exile and death, if it were to be immediately adopted, and were to continue in force, not until a BETTER, but until ANOTHER should be agreed upon by this new assembly of lawgivers.

It is a matter both of wonder and regret that those who raise so many objections against the new Constitution should never call to mind the defects of that which is to be exchanged for it. It is not necessary that the former should be perfect: it is sufficient that the latter is more imperfect. No man would refuse to give brass for silver or gold, because the latter had some alloy in it. No man would refuse to quit a shattered and tottering habitation for a firm and commodious building, because the latter had not a porch to it, or because some of the rooms might be a little larger or smaller, or the ceiling a little higher or lower than his fancy would have planned them. But waiving illustrations of this sort, is it not manifest that most of the capital objections urged against the new system lie with tenfold weight against the existing Confederation? Is an indefinite power to raise money dangerous in the hands of a federal government? The present Congress can make requisitions to any amount they please, and the states are constitutionally bound to furnish them; they can emit bills of credit as long as they will pay for the paper; they can borrow, both abroad and at home, as long as a shilling will be lent. Is an indefinite power to raise troops dangerous? The Confederation gives to Congress that power also; and they have already begun to make use of it. Is it improper and unsafe to intermix the different powers of government in the same body of men? Congress, a single body of men, are the sole depositary of all the federal powers. Is it particularly dangerous to give the keys of the treasury, and the command of the army, into the same hands? The Confederation places them both in the hands of Congress. Is a bill of rights essential to liberty? The Confederation has no bill of rights. Is it an objection against the new Constitution that it empowers the Senate, with the concurrence of the Executive, to make treaties which are to be the laws of the land? The existing Congress, without any such control, can make treaties which they themselves have declared, and most of the states have recognized, to be the supreme law of the land. Is the importation of slaves permitted by the new Constitution for twenty years? By the old it is permitted forever.

I shall be told that however dangerous this mixture of powers may be in theory, it is rendered harmless by the dependence of Congress on the states for the means of carrying them into practice; that however large the mass of powers may be, it is in fact a lifeless mass. Then, say I, in the first place, that the Confederation is chargeable with the still greater folly of declaring certain powers in the federal government to be absolutely necessary, and at the same time rendering them absolutely nugatory; and, in the next place, that if the Union is to continue, and no better government be substituted, effective powers must either be granted to, or assumed by, the existing Congress; in either of which events, the contrast just stated will hold good. But this is not all. Out of this lifeless mass has already grown an excrescent power, which tends to realize all the dangers that can be apprehended from a defective construction of the supreme government of the Union. It is now no longer a point of speculation and hope that the Western territory is a mine of vast wealth to the United States; and although it is not of such a nature as to extricate them from their present distresses, or, for some time to come, to yield any regular supplies for the public expenses, yet must it hereafter be able, under proper management, both to effect a gradual discharge of the domestic debt, and to furnish, for a certain period, liberal tributes to the federal treasury. A very large proportion of this fund has been already surrendered by individual states; and it may with reason be expected that the remaining states will not persist in withholding similar proofs of their equity and generosity. We may calculate, therefore, that a rich and fertile country, of an area equal to the inhabited extent of the United States, will soon become a national stock. Congress have assumed the administration of this stock. They have begun to render it productive. Congress have undertaken to do more: they have proceeded to form new states, to erect temporary governments, to appoint officers for them, and to prescribe the conditions on which such states shall be admitted into the Confederacy. All this has been done, and done without the least color of constitutional authority. Yet no blame has been whispered; no alarm has been sounded. A GREAT and INDEPENDENT fund of revenue is passing into the hands of a SINGLE BODY of men, who can RAISE TROOPS to an INDEFINITE NUMBER, and appropriate money to their support for an INDEFINITE PERIOD OF TIME. And yet there are men who have not only been silent spectators of this prospect, but who are advocates for the system which exhibits it; and, at the same time, urge against the new system the objections which we have heard. Would they not act with more consistency, in urging the establishment of the latter, as no less necessary to guard the Union against the future powers and resources of a body constructed like the existing Congress, than to save it from the dangers threatened by the present impotency of that assembly?

I mean not, by anything here said, to throw censure on the measures which have been pursued by Congress. I am sensible they could not have done otherwise. The public interest, the necessity of the case, imposed upon them the task of overleaping their constitutional limits. But is not the fact an alarming proof of the danger resulting from a government which does not possess regular powers commensurate to its objects? A dissolution or usurpation is the dreadful dilemma to which it is continually exposed.

PUBLIUS.

V

THE CONFORMITY OF THE NEW CONSTITUTION TO REPUBLICAN PRINCIPLES

ESTABLISHES A GOVERNMENT BOTH REPUBLICAN AND FEDERAL

The Conformity of the Plan to Republican Principles: an Objection in Respect to the Powers of the Convention examined [1]

The last paper having concluded the observations which were meant to introduce a candid survey of the plan of government reported by the Convention, we now proceed to the execution of that part of our undertaking.

The first question that offers itself is, whether the general form and aspect of the government be strictly republican. It is evident that no other form would be reconcilable with the genius of the people of America; with the fundamental principles of the Revolution; or with that honorable determination which animates every votary of freedom, to rest all our political experiments on the capacity of mankind for self-government. If the plan of the Convention, therefore, be found to depart from the republican character, its advocates must abandon it as no longer defensible.

What, then, are the distinctive characters of the republican form? Were an answer to this question to be sought, not by recurring to principles, but in the application of the term by political writers, to the constitutions of different states, no satisfactory one would ever be found. Holland, in which no particle of the supreme authority is derived from the people, has passed almost universally under the denomination of a republic. The same title has been bestowed on Venice, where absolute

[1] No. XXXIX (XXXVIII). Madison. Independent Journal, January 16, 1788.

power over the great body of the people is exercised, in the most absolute manner, by a small body of hereditary nobles. Poland, which is a mixture of aristocracy and of monarchy in their worst forms, has been dignified with the same appellation. The government of England, which has one republican branch only, combined with an hereditary aristocracy and monarchy, has, with equal impropriety, been frequently placed on the list of republics. These examples, which are nearly as dissimilar to each other as to a genuine republic, show the extreme inaccuracy with which the term has been used in political disquisitions.

If we resort for a criterion to the different principles on which different forms of government are established, we may define a republic to be, or at least may bestow that name on, a government which derives all its powers directly or indirectly from the great body of the people, and is administered by persons holding their offices during pleasure, for a limited period, or during good behavior. It is *essential* to such a government that it be derived from the great body of the society, not from an inconsiderable proportion, or a favored class of it; otherwise a handful of tyrannical nobles, exercising their oppressions by a delegation of their powers, might aspire to the rank of republicans, and claim for their government the honorable title of republic. It is *sufficient* for such a government that the persons administering it be appointed, either directly or indirectly, by the people; and that they hold their appointments by either of the tenures just specified; otherwise every government in the United States, as well as every other popular government that has been or can be well organized or well executed, would be degraded from the republican character. According to the constitution of every state in the Union, some or other of the officers of government are appointed indirectly only by the people. According to most of them, the chief magistrate himself is so appointed. And according to one, this mode of appointment is extended to one of the coördinate branches of the legislature. According to all the constitutions, also, the tenure of the highest offices is extended to a definite period, and in many instances, both within the legislative and executive departments, to a period of years. According to the provisions of most of the constitutions, again, as well as according to the most respectable and received opinions on the subject, the members of the judiciary department are to retain their offices by the firm tenure of good behavior.

On comparing the Constitution planned by the Convention with the standard here fixed, we perceive at once that it is, in the most rigid sense, conformable to it. The House of Representatives, like that of one branch at least of all the state legislatures, is elected immediately by the great body of the people. The Senate, like the present Congress, and the senate of Maryland, derives its appointment indirectly from the people. The President is indirectly derived from the choice of the people, according to the example in most of the states. Even the judges, with all other officers of the Union, will, as in the several states, be the choice, though a remote choice, of the people themselves. The duration of the appointments is equally conformable to the republican standard, and to the model of the state constitutions. The House of Representatives is periodically elective, as in all the states, and for the period of two years, as in the state of South Carolina. The Senate is elective for the period of six years, which is but one year more than the period of the senate of Maryland, and but two more than that of the senates of New York and Virginia. The President is to continue in office for the period of four years; as in New York and Delaware the chief magistrate is elected for three years, and in South Carolina for two years. In the other states the election is annual. In several of the states, however, no explicit provision is made for the impeachment of the chief magistrate. And in Delaware and Virginia he is not impeachable till out of office. The President of the United States is impeachable at any time during his continuance in office. The tenure by which the judges are to hold their places is, as it unquestionably ought to be, that of good behavior. The tenure of the ministerial offices generally will be a subject of legal regulation, conformably to the reason of the case and the example of the state constitutions.

Could any further proof be required of the republican complexion of this system, the most decisive one might be found in its absolute prohibition of titles of nobility, both under the federal and the state governments, and in its express guarantee of the republican form to each of the latter.

But it was not sufficient, say the adversaries of the proposed Constitution, for the Convention to adhere to the republican form. They ought, with equal care, to have preserved the *federal* form, which regards the Union as a *confederacy* of sovereign states; instead of which, they have framed a *national* government, which regards the Union as a *consolidation* of the states. And it is asked by what authority this bold and radical innovation was undertaken? The handle which has been made of this objection requires that it should be examined with some precision.

Without inquiring into the accuracy of the distinction on which the objection is founded, it will be necessary to a just estimate of its force, first, to ascertain the real character of the government in question; secondly, to inquire how far the Convention were authorized to propose such a government; and thirdly, how far the duty they owed to their country could supply any defect of regular authority.

First: In order to ascertain the real character of the government, it may be considered in relation to the foundation on which it is to be established; to the sources from which its ordinary powers are to be drawn; to the operation of those powers; to the extent of them; and to the authority by which future changes in the government are to be introduced.

On examining the first relation, it appears, on one hand, that the Constitution is to be founded on the assent and ratification of the people of America, given by deputies elected for the special purpose; but, on the other, that this assent and ratification is to be given by the people, not as individuals composing one entire nation, but as composing the distinct and independent states to which they respectively belong. It is to be the assent and ratification of the several states, derived from the supreme authority in each state, — the authority of the people themselves. The act, therefore, establishing the Constitution will not be a *national*, but a *federal* act.

That it will be a federal and not a national act, as these terms are understood by the objectors, the act of the people, as forming so many independent states, not as forming one aggregate nation, is obvious from this single consideration, that it is to result neither from the decision of a *majority* of the people of the Union, nor from that of a *majority* of the states. It must result from the *unanimous* assent of the several states that are parties to it, differing no otherwise from their ordinary assent than in its being expressed, not by the legislative authority, but by that of the people themselves. Were the people regarded in this transaction as forming one nation, the will of the majority of the whole people of the United States would bind the minority, in the same manner as the majority in each state must bind the minority; and the will of the majority must be determined either by a comparison of the individual votes, or by considering the will of the majority of the states as evidence of the will of a majority of the people of the United States. Neither of these rules has been adopted. Each state, in ratifying the Constitution, is considered as a sovereign body, independent of all others and only to be bound by its own voluntary act. In this relation, then, the new Constitution will, if established, be a *federal*, and not a *national*, constitution.

The next relation is to the sources from which the ordinary powers of government are to be derived. The House of Representatives will derive its powers from the people of America; and the people will be represented in the same proportion, and on the same principle, as they are in the legislature of a particular state. So far the government is *national*, not *federal*. The Senate, on the other hand, will derive its powers from the states, as political and coequal societies; and these will be represented on the principle of equality in the Senate, as they now are in the existing Congress. So far the government is *federal*, not *national*. The executive power will be derived from a very compound source. The immediate election of the President is to be made by the states in their political characters. The votes allotted to them are in a compound ratio, which considers them partly as distinct and coequal societies, partly as unequal members of the same society. The eventual election, again, is to be made by that branch of the legislature which consists of the national representatives; but in this particular act they are to be thrown into the form of individual delegations, from so many distinct and coequal bodies politic. From this aspect of the government, it appears to be of a mixed character, presenting at least as many *federal* as *national* features.

The difference between a federal and national government, as it relates to the *operation of the government*, is by the adversaries of the plan of the Convention supposed to consist in this, that in the former the powers operate on the political bodies composing the Confederacy, in their political capacities; in the latter, on the individual citizens composing the nation, in their individual capacities. On trying the Constitution by this criterion, it falls under the *national*, not the *federal* character, though perhaps not so completely as has been understood. In several cases, and particularly in the trial of controversies to which states may be parties, they must be viewed and proceeded against in their collective and political capacities only. But the operation of the government on the people, in their individual capacities, in its ordinary and most essential proceedings, will, on the whole, in the sense of its opponents, designate it, in this relation, a *national* government.

But if the government be national with regard to the *operation* of its powers, it changes its aspect again when we contemplate it in relation to the *extent* of its powers. The idea of a national government involves in it, not only an authority over the individual citizens, but an indefinite supremacy over all persons and things, so far as they are objects of lawful government. Among a people consolidated into one nation, this supremacy is completely vested in the national legislature. Among communities united for particular purposes, it is vested partly in the general and partly in the municipal legislatures. In the former case, all local authorities are subordinate to the supreme; and may be controlled, directed, or abolished by it at pleasure. In the latter, the local or municipal authorities form distinct and independent portions of the supremacy, no more subject, within their respective spheres, to the general authority than the general authority is subject to them within its own sphere. In this relation, then, the proposed government cannot be deemed a *national* one, since its jurisdiction extends to certain enumerated objects only, and leaves to the several states a residuary and inviolable sovereignty over all other objects. It is true that in controversies relating to the boundary between the two jurisdictions, the tribunal which is ultimately to decide, is to be established under the general government. But this does not change the principle of the case. The decision is to be impartially made, according to the rules of the Constitution; and all the usual and most effectual precautions are taken to secure this impartiality. Some such tribunal is clearly essential to prevent an appeal to the sword and a dissolution of the compact; and that it ought to be established under the general rather than under the local governments, or, to speak more properly, that it could be safely established under the first alone, is a position not likely to be combated.

If we try the Constitution by its last relation to the authority by which amendments are to be made, we find it neither wholly *national* nor wholly *federal*. Were it wholly national, the supreme and ultimate authority would reside in the *majority* of the people of the Union; and this authority would be competent at all times, like that of a majority of every national society, to alter or abolish its established government. Were it wholly federal, on the other hand, the concurrence of each state in the Union would be essential to every alteration that would be binding on all. The mode provided by the plan of the Convention is not founded on either of these principles. In requiring more than a majority, and particularly in computing the proportion by *states*, not by *citizens*, it departs from the *national* and advances towards the *federal* character; in rendering the concurrence of less than the whole number of states sufficient, it loses again the *federal* and partakes of the *national* character.

The proposed Constitution, therefore, even when tested by the rules laid down by its antagonists, is, in strictness, neither a national nor a federal Constitution, but a composition of both. In its foundation it is federal, not national; in the sources from which the ordinary powers of the government are drawn, it is partly federal and partly national; in the operation of these powers, it is national, not federal; in the extent of them, again, it is federal, not national; and, finally, in the authoritative mode of introducing amendments, it is neither wholly federal nor wholly national.

PUBLIUS.

VI

JUSTIFICATION OF THE POWERS CONFERRED BY THE NEW CONSTITUTION UPON THE FEDERAL GOVERNMENT

(a) MILITARY POWERS

General View of the Powers proposed to be vested in the Union[1]

The Constitution proposed by the Convention may be considered under two general points of view. The *first* relates to the sum or quantity of power which it vests in the government, including the restraints imposed on the states. The *second*, to the particular structure of the government, and the distribution of this power among its several branches.

Under the first view of the subject, two important questions arise: 1. Whether any part of the powers transferred to the general government be unnecessary or improper? 2. Whether the entire mass of them be dangerous to the portion of jurisdiction left in the several states?

Is the aggregate power of the general government greater than ought to have been vested in it? This is the first question.

It cannot have escaped those who have attended with candor to the arguments employed against the extensive powers of the government, that the authors of them have very little considered how far these powers were necessary means of attaining a necessary end. They have chosen rather to dwell on the inconveniences which must be unavoidably blended with all political advantages, and on the possible abuses which must be incident to every power or trust, of which a beneficial use can be made. This method of handling the subject cannot impose on the good sense of the people of America. It may display the subtlety

[1] No. XLI (XL). Madison. Independent Journal, January 19, 1788.

of the writer, it may open a boundless field for rhetoric and declamation, it may inflame the passions of the unthinking, and may confirm the prejudices of the misthinking; but cool and candid people will at once reflect that the purest of human blessings must have a portion of alloy in them; that the choice must always be made, if not of the lesser evil, at least of the GREATER, not the PERFECT, good; and that in every political institution, a power to advance the public happiness involves a discretion which may be misapplied and abused. They will see, therefore, that in all cases where power is to be conferred, the point first to be decided is, whether such a power be necessary to the public good; as the next will be, in case of an affirmative decision, to guard as effectually as possible against a perversion of the power to the public detriment.

That we may form a correct judgment on this subject, it will be proper to review the several powers conferred on the government of the Union; and that this may be the more conveniently done they may be reduced into different classes as they relate to the following different objects: 1. Security against foreign danger. 2. Regulation of the intercourse with foreign nations. 3. Maintenance of harmony and proper intercourse among the states. 4. Certain miscellaneous objects of general utility. 5. Restraint of the states from certain injurious acts. 6. Provisions for giving due efficacy to all these powers.

The powers falling within the first class are those of declaring war and granting letters of marque; of providing armies and fleets; of regulating and calling forth the militia; of levying and borrowing money.

Security against foreign danger is one of the primitive objects of civil society. It is an avowed and essential object of the American Union. The powers requisite for attaining it must be effectually confided to the federal councils.

Is the power of declaring war necessary? No man will answer this question in the negative. It would be superfluous, therefore, to enter into a proof of the affirmative. The existing confederation establishes this power in the most ample form.

Is the power of raising armies and equipping fleets necessary? This is involved in the foregoing power. It is involved in the power of self-defense.

But was it necessary to give an INDEFINITE POWER of raising TROOPS, as well as providing fleets; and of maintaining both in PEACE, as well as in WAR?

The answer to these questions has been too far anticipated in another place to admit an extensive discussion of them in this place. The answer indeed seems to be so obvious and conclusive as scarcely to justify such a discussion in any place. With what color of propriety could the force necessary for defense be limited by those who cannot limit the force of offense? If a federal Constitution could chain the ambition or set bounds to the exertions of all other nations, then indeed might it prudently chain the discretion of its own government, and set bounds to the exertions for its own safety.

How could a readiness for war in time of peace be safely prohibited, unless we could prohibit, in like manner, the preparations and establishments of every hostile nation? The means of security can only be regulated by the means and the danger of attack. They will, in fact, be ever determined by these rules, and by no others. It is in vain to oppose constitutional barriers to the impulse of self-preservation. It is worse than in vain; because it plants in the Constitution itself necessary usurpations of power, every precedent of which is a germ of unnecessary and multiplied repetitions. If one nation maintains constantly a disciplined army, ready for the service of ambition or revenge, it obliges the most pacific nations who may be within the reach of its enterprises to take corresponding precautions. The fifteenth century was the unhappy epoch of military establishments in time of peace. They were introduced by Charles VII of France. All Europe has followed, or been forced into, the example. Had the example not been followed by other nations all Europe must long ago have worn the chains of a universal monarch. Were every nation except France now to disband its peace establishment, the same event might follow.

The veteran legions of Rome were an overmatch for the undisciplined valor of all other nations, and rendered her mistress of the world.

Not less true is it, that the liberties of Rome proved the final victim to her military triumphs; and that the liberties of Europe, as far as they ever existed, have, with few exceptions, been the price of her military establishments. A standing force, therefore, is a dangerous, at the same time that it may be a necessary provision. On the smallest scale it has its inconveniences. On an extensive scale its consequences may be fatal. On any scale it is an object of laudable circumspection and precaution. A wise nation will combine all these considerations; and, whilst it does not rashly preclude itself from any resource which may become essential to its safety, will exert all its prudence in diminishing both the necessity and the danger of resorting to one which may be inauspicious to its liberties.

The clearest marks of this prudence are stamped on the proposed Constitution. The Union itself, which it cements and secures, destroys every pretext for a military establishment which could be dangerous. America united, with a handful of troops, or without a single soldier, exhibits a more forbidding posture to foreign ambition than America disunited, with an hundred thousand veterans ready for combat. It was remarked on a former occasion, that the want of this pretext had saved the liberties of one nation in Europe. Being rendered by her insular situation and her maritime resources impregnable to the armies of her neighbors, the rulers of Great Britain have never been able, by real or artificial dangers, to cheat the public into an extensive peace establishment. The distance of the United States from the powerful nations of the world gives them the same happy security. A dangerous establishment can never be necessary or plausible, so long as they continue a united people. But let it never, for a moment, be forgotten that they are indebted for this advantage to their union alone. The moment of its dissolution will be the date of a new order of things. The fears of the weaker, or the ambition of the stronger states, or confederacies, will set the same example in the New as Charles VII did in the Old World. The example will be followed here from the same motives which produced universal imitation there. Instead of deriving from our situation the precious advantage which Great Britain has derived from hers, the face of America will be but a copy of that of the continent of Europe. It will present liberty everywhere crushed between standing armies and perpetual taxes. The fortunes of disunited America will be even more disastrous than those of Europe. The sources of evil in the latter are confined to her own limits. No superior powers of another quarter of the globe intrigue among her rival nations, inflame their mutual animosities and render them the instruments of foreign ambition, jealousy, and revenge. In America the miseries springing from her internal jealousies, contentions, and wars would form a part only of her lot. A plentiful addition of evils would have their source in that relation in which Europe stands to this quarter of the earth, and which no other quarter of the earth bears to Europe.

This picture of the consequences of disunion cannot be too highly colored, or too often exhibited. Every man who loves peace, every man who loves his country, every man who loves liberty, ought to have it ever before his eyes, that he may cherish in his heart a due attachment to the union of America, and be able to set a due value on the means of preserving it.

Next to the effectual establishment of the Union, the best possible precaution against danger from standing armies is a limitation of the term for which revenue may be appropriated to their support. This precaution the Constitution has prudently added. I will not repeat here the observations which I flatter myself have placed this subject in a just and satisfactory light. But it may not be improper to take notice of an argument against this part of the Constitution which has been drawn from the policy and practice of Great Britain. It is said that the continuance of an army in that kingdom requires an annual vote of the legislature; whereas the American Constitution has lengthened this critical period to two years. This is the form in which the comparison is usually stated to the public: but is it a just form? Is it a fair comparison? Does the British Constitution restrain the parliamentary discretion to one year? Does the American impose on the Congress appropriations for two years? On the contrary, it cannot be unknown to the authors of the fallacy themselves, that the British Constitution fixes no limit whatever to the discretion of the legislature, and that the American ties down the legislature to two years, as the longest admissible term.

Had the argument from the British example been truly stated, it would have stood thus: The term for which supplies may be appropriated to the army establishment, though unlimited by the British Constitution, has nevertheless, in practice, been limited by parliamentary discretion to a single year. Now, if in Great Britain, where the House of Commons is elected for seven years, where so great a proportion of the members are elected by so small a proportion of the people, where the electors are so corrupted by the representatives, and the representatives so corrupted by the crown, the representative body can possess a power to make appropriations to the army for an indefinite term, without desiring, or without daring, to extend the term beyond a single year, ought not suspicion herself to blush, in pretending that the representatives of the United States, elected FREELY by the WHOLE BODY of the people, every SECOND YEAR, cannot be safely intrusted with the discretion over such appropriations, expressly limited to the short period of TWO YEARS?

A bad cause seldom fails to betray itself. Of this truth, the management of the opposition to the federal government is an unvaried exemplification. But among all the blunders which have been committed, none is more striking than the attempt to enlist on that side the prudent jealousy entertained by the people of standing armies. The attempt has awakened fully the public attention to that important subject, and has led to investigations which must terminate in a thorough and universal conviction, not only that the Constitution has provided the most effectual guards against danger from that quarter, but that nothing short of a Constitution fully adequate to the national defense and the preservation of the Union can save America from as many standing armies as it may be split into states or confederacies, and from such a progressive augmentation of these establishments in each as will render them as burdensome to the properties and ominous to the liberties of the people as any establishment that can become necessary, under a united and efficient government, must be tolerable to the former and safe to the latter.

The palpable necessity of the power to provide and maintain a navy has protected that part of the Constitution against a spirit of censure, which has spared few other parts. It must, indeed, be numbered among the greatest blessings of America, that as her Union will be the only source of her maritime strength, so this will be a principal source of her security against danger from abroad. In this respect our situation bears another likeness to the insular advantage of Great Britain. The batteries most capable of repelling foreign enterprises on our safety are happily such as can never be turned by a perfidious government against our liberties.

The inhabitants of the Atlantic frontier are all of them deeply interested in this provision for naval protection, and if they have hitherto been suffered to sleep quietly in their beds, if their property has remained safe against the predatory spirit of licentious adventurers, if their maritime towns have not yet been compelled to ransom themselves from the terrors of a conflagration, by yielding to the exactions of daring and sudden invaders, these instances of good fortune are not to be ascribed to the capacity of the existing government for the protection of those from whom it claims allegiance, but to causes that are fugitive and fallacious. If we except perhaps Virginia and Maryland, which are peculiarly vulnerable on their eastern frontiers, no part of the Union ought to feel more anxiety on this subject than New York. Her seacoast is extensive. The very important district of the state is an island. The state itself is penetrated by a large navigable river for more than fifty leagues. The great emporium of its commerce, the great reservoir of its wealth, lies every moment at the mercy of events, and may almost be regarded as a hostage for ignominious compliances with the dictates of a foreign enemy, or even with the rapacious demands of pirates and barbarians. Should a war be the result of the precarious situation of European affairs, and all the unruly passions attending it be let loose on the ocean, our escape from insults and depredations, not only on that element, but every part of the other bordering on it, will be truly miraculous. In the present condition of America, the states more immediately exposed to these calamities have nothing to hope from the phantom of a general government which now exists; and if their single resources were equal to the task of fortifying themselves against the danger, the object to be protected would be almost consumed by the means of protecting them.

The power of regulating and calling forth the militia has been already sufficiently vindicated and explained.

The power of levying and borrowing money, being the sinew of that which is to be exerted in the national defense, is properly thrown into the same class with it. This power, also, has been examined already with much attention, and has, I trust, been clearly shown to be necessary, both in the extent and form given to it by the Constitution. I will address one additional reflection only to those who contend that the power ought to have been restrained to external taxation — by which they mean taxes on articles imported from other countries. It cannot be doubted that this will always be a valuable source of revenue; that for a considerable time it must be a principal source; that at this moment it is an essential one. But we may form very mistaken ideas on this subject if we do not call to mind in our calculations that the extent of revenue drawn from foreign commerce must vary with the variations, both in the extent and the kind of imports; and that these variations do not correspond with the progress of population, which must be the general measure of the public wants. A long as agriculture continues the sole field of labor, the importation of manufactures must increase as the consumers multiply. As soon as domestic manufactures are begun by the hands not called for by agriculture, the imported manufactures will decrease as the numbers of people increase. In a more remote stage, the imports may consist in considerable part of raw materials, which will be wrought into articles for exportation, and will, therefore, require rather the encouragement of bounties than to be loaded with discouraging duties. A system of government, meant for duration, ought to contemplate these revolutions, and be able to accommodate itself to them.

Some, who have not denied the necessity of the power of taxation, have grounded a very fierce attack against the Constitution on the language in which it is defined. It has been urged and echoed that the power "to lay and collect taxes, duties, imposts and excises, to pay the debts, and provide for the common defence and general welfare of the United States," amounts to an unlimited commission to exercise every power which may be alleged to be necessary for the common defense or general welfare. No stronger proof could be given of the distress under which these writers labor for objections, than their stooping to such a misconstruction.

Had no other enumeration or definition of the powers of the Congress been found in the Constitution than the general expressions just cited, the authors of the objection might have had some color for it; though it would have been difficult to find a reason for so awkward a form of describing an authority to legislate in all possible cases. A power to destroy the freedom of the press, the trial by jury, or even to regulate the course of descents, or the forms of conveyances, must be very singularly expressed by the terms "to raise money for the general welfare."

But what color can the objection have when a specification of the objects alluded to by these general terms immediately follows, and is not even separated by a longer pause than a semicolon? If the different parts of the same instrument ought to be so expounded, as to give meaning to every part which will bear it, shall one part of the same sentence be excluded altogether from a share in the meaning; and shall the more doubtful and indefinite terms be retained in their full extent, and the clear and precise expressions be denied any signification whatsoever? For what purpose could the enumeration of particular powers be inserted, if these and all others were meant to be included in the preceding general power? Nothing is more natural or common than first to use a general phrase, and then to explain and qualify it by a recital of particulars. But the idea of an enumeration of particulars which neither explain nor qualify the general meaning, and can have no other effect than to confound and mislead, is an absurdity, which, as we are reduced to the dilemma of charging either on the authors of the objection or on the authors of the Constitution, we must take the liberty of supposing, had not its origin with the latter.

The objection here is the more extraordinary, as it appears that the language used by the Convention is a copy from the Articles of Confederation. The objects of the Union among the states, as described in article third, are, "their common defence, security of their liberties, and mutual and general welfare." The terms of article eighth are still more identical: "All charges of war, and all other expenses, that shall be incurred for the common defence or general welfare, and allowed by the United States in Congress shall be defrayed out of a common treasury," etc. A similar language again occurs in article ninth. Construe either of these articles by the rules which would justify the construction put on the new Constitution, and they vest in the existing Congress a power to legislate in all cases whatsoever. But what would have been thought of that assembly, if, attaching themselves to these general expressions, and disregarding the specifications which ascertain and limit their import, they had exercised an unlimited power of providing for the common defense and general welfare? I appeal to the objectors themselves, whether they would in that case have employed the same reasoning in justification of Congress as they now make use of against the Convention. How difficult it is for error to escape its own condemnation! PUBLIUS.

(b) DIPLOMATIC AND COMMERCIAL POWERS

The same View continued[1]

The *second* class of powers, lodged in the general government, consists of those which regulate the intercourse with foreign nations, to wit: to make treaties; to send and receive ambassadors, other public ministers, and consuls; to define and punish piracies and felonies committed on the high seas, and offenses against the law of nations; to regulate foreign commerce, including a power to prohibit, after the year 1808, the importation of slaves, and to lay an intermediate duty of ten dollars per head, as a discouragement to such importations.

This class of powers forms an obvious and essential branch of the federal administration. If we are to be one nation in any respect, it clearly ought to be in respect to other nations.

The powers to make treaties and to send and receive ambassadors speak their own propriety. Both of them are comprised in the Articles of Confederation, with this difference only, that the former is disembarrassed, by the plan of the Convention, of an exception, under which treaties might be substantially frustrated by regulations of the states; and that a power of appointing and receiving "other public ministers and consuls," is expressly and very properly added to the former provision concerning ambassadors. The term ambassador, if taken strictly, as seems to be required by the second of the Articles of Confederation, comprehends the highest grade only of public ministers, and excludes the grades which the United States will be most likely to prefer, where foreign embassies may be necessary. And under no latitude of construction will the term comprehend consuls. Yet it has been found expedient, and has been the practice of Congress, to employ the inferior grades of public ministers, and to send and receive consuls.

It is true that where treaties of commerce stipulate for the mutual appointment of consuls, whose functions are connected with commerce, the admission of foreign consuls may fall within

[1] No. XLII (XLI). Madison. New York Packet, January 22, 1788.

the power of making commercial treaties; and that where no such treaties exist, the mission of American consuls into foreign countries may *perhaps* be covered under the authority, given by the ninth article of the Confederation, to appoint all such civil officers as may be necessary for managing the general affairs of the United States. But the admission of consuls into the United States, where no previous treaty has stipulated it, seems to have been nowhere provided for. A supply of the omission is one of the lesser instances in which the Convention have improved on the model before them. But the most minute provisions become important when they tend to obviate the necessity or the pretext for gradual and unobserved usurpations of power. A list of the cases in which Congress have been betrayed, or forced by the defects of the Confederation, into violations of their chartered authorities, would not a little surprise those who have paid no attention to the subject; and would be no inconsiderable argument in favor of the new Constitution, which seems to have provided no less studiously for the lesser, than the more obvious and striking defects of the old.

The power to define and punish piracies and felonies committed on the high seas, and offenses against the law of nations, belongs with equal propriety to the general government, and is a still greater improvement on the Articles of Confederation. These articles contain no provision for the case of offenses against the law of nations, and consequently leave it in the power of any indiscreet member to embroil the Confederacy with foreign nations. The provision of the federal articles on the subject of piracies and felonies extends no further than to the establishment of courts for the trial of these offenses. The definition of piracies might, perhaps, without inconveniency, be left to the law of nations; though a legislative definition of them is found in most municipal codes. A definition of felonies on the high seas is evidently requisite. Felony is a term of loose signification, even in the common law of England, and of various import in the statute law of that kingdom. But neither the common nor the statute law of that, or of any other nation, ought to be a standard for the proceedings of this, unless previously made its own by legislative adoption. The meaning of the term, as defined in the codes of the several states, would be as impracticable as the former would be a dishonorable and illegitimate guide. It is not precisely the same in any two of the states, and varies in each with every revision of its criminal laws. For the sake of certainty and uniformity, therefore, the power of defining felonies in this case was in every respect necessary and proper.

The regulation of foreign commerce, having fallen within several views which have been taken of this subject, has been too fully discussed to need additional proofs here of its being properly submitted to the federal administration.

It were doubtless to be wished that the power of prohibiting the importation of slaves had not been postponed until the year 1808, or rather that it had been suffered to have immediate operation. But it is not difficult to account, either for this restriction on the general government, or for the manner in which the whole clause is expressed. It ought to be considered as a great point gained in favor of humanity, that a period of twenty years may terminate forever, within these states, a traffic which has so long and so loudly upbraided the barbarism of modern policy; that within that period it will receive a considerable discouragement from the federal government, and may be totally abolished by a concurrence of the few states which continue the unnatural traffic in the prohibitory example which has been given by so great a majority of the Union. Happy would it be for the unfortunate Africans, if an equal prospect lay before them of being redeemed from the oppressions of their European brethren!

Attempts have been made to pervert this clause into an objection against the Constitution, by representing it on one side as a criminal toleration of an illicit practice, and on another as calculated to prevent voluntary and beneficial emigrations from Europe to America. I mention these misconstructions, not with a view to give them an answer, for they deserve none, but as specimens of the manner and spirit in which some have thought fit to conduct their opposition to the proposed government.

The powers included in the *third* class are those which provide for the harmony and proper intercourse among the states.

Under this head might be included the particular restraints imposed on the authority of the states, and certain powers of the judicial department; but the former are reserved for a distinct class, and the latter will be particularly examined when we arrive at the structure and organization of the government. I shall confine myself to a cursory review of the remaining powers comprehended under this third description, to wit: to regulate commerce among the several states and the Indian tribes; to coin money, regulate the value thereof, and of foreign coin; to provide for the punishment of counterfeiting the current coin and securities of the United States; to fix the standard of weights and measures; to establish a uniform rule of naturalization, and uniform laws of bankruptcy; to prescribe the manner in which the public acts, records, and judicial proceedings of each state shall be proved, and the effect they shall have in other states; and to establish post-offices and post-roads.

The defect of power in the existing Confederacy to regulate the commerce between its several members is in the number of those which have been clearly pointed out by experience. To the proofs and remarks which former papers have brought into view on this subject, it may be added that, without this supplemental provision, the great and essential power of regulating foreign commerce would have been incomplete and ineffectual. A very material object of this power was the relief of the states which import and export through other states from the improper contributions levied on them by the latter. Were these at liberty to regulate the trade between state and state, it must be foreseen that ways would be found out to load the articles of import and export, during the passage through their jurisdiction, with duties which would fall on the makers of the latter and the consumers of the former. We may be assured by past experience that such a practice would be introduced by future contrivances; and both by that and a common knowledge of human affairs, that it would nourish unceasing animosities and not improbably terminate in serious interruptions of the public tranquillity. To those who do not view the question through the medium of passion or of interest, the desire of the commercial states to collect, in any form, an indirect revenue from their uncommercial neighbors, must appear not less impolitic than it is unfair; since it would stimulate the injured party, by resentment as well as interest, to resort to less convenient channels for their foreign trade. But the mild voice of reason, pleading the cause of an enlarged and permanent interest, is but too often drowned, before public bodies as well as individuals, by the clamors of an impatient avidity for immediate and immoderate gain.

The necessity of a superintending authority over the reciprocal trade of confederated states has been illustrated by other examples as well as our own. In Switzerland, where the union is so very slight, each canton is obliged to allow to merchandises a passage through its jurisdiction into other cantons, without an augmentation of the tolls. In Germany it is a law of the empire that the princes and states shall not lay tolls or customs on bridges, rivers, or passages, without the consent of the emperor and diet; though it appears from a quotation in an antecedent paper that the practice in this, as in many other instances in that confederacy, has not followed the law, and has produced there the mischiefs which have been foreseen here. Among the restraints imposed by the union of the Netherlands on its members, one is, that they shall not establish imposts disadvantageous to their neighbors, without the general permission.

The regulation of commerce with the Indian tribes is very properly unfettered from two limitations in the Articles of Confederation, which render the provision obscure and contradictory.

The power is there restrained to Indians, not members of any of the states, and is not to violate or infringe the legislative right of any state within its own limits. What description of Indians are to be deemed members of a state is not yet settled, and has been a question of frequent perplexity and contention in the federal councils. And how the trade with Indians, though not members of a state, yet residing within its legislative jurisdiction, can be regulated by an external authority, without so far intruding on the internal rights of legislation, is absolutely incomprehensible. This is not the only case in which the Articles of Confederation have inconsiderately endeavored to accomplish impossibilities; to reconcile a partial sovereignty in the Union with complete sovereignty in the states; to subvert a mathematical axiom by taking away a part, and letting the whole remain.

All that need be remarked on the power to coin money, regulate the value thereof, and of foreign coin, is, that by providing for this last case, the Constitution has supplied a material omission in the Articles of Confederation. The authority of the existing Congress is restrained to the regulation of coin *struck* by their own authority, or that of the respective states. It must be seen at once that the proposed uniformity in the *value* of the current coin might be destroyed by subjecting that of foreign coin to the different regulations of the different states.

The punishment of counterfeiting the public securities, as well as of the current coin, is submitted of course to that authority which is to secure the value of both.

The regulation of weights and measures is transferred from the Articles of Confederation, and is founded on like considerations with the preceding power of regulating coin.

The dissimilarity in the rules of naturalization has long been remarked as a fault in our system, and as laying a foundation for intricate and delicate questions. In the fourth article of the Confederation it is declared "that the *free inhabitants* of each of these states, paupers, vagabonds, and fugitives from justice excepted, shall be entitled to all privileges and immunities of *free citizens*, in the several states, and *the people* of each state shall, in every other, enjoy all the privileges of trade and commerce," etc. There is a confusion of language here which is remarkable. Why the terms *free inhabitants* are used in one part of the article, *free citizens* in another, and *people* in another, or what was meant by superadding to "all privileges and immunities of free citizens," "all the privileges of trade and commerce," cannot easily be determined. It seems to be a construction scarcely avoidable, however, that those who come under the denomination of *free inhabitants* of a state, although not citizens of such state, are entitled, in every other state, to all the privileges of *free citizens* of the latter; that is, to greater privileges than they may be entitled to in their own state; so that it may be in the power of a particular state, or rather every state is laid under a necessity, not only to confer the rights of citizenship in other states upon any whom it may admit to such rights within itself, but upon any whom it may allow to become inhabitants within its jurisdiction. But were an exposition of the term "inhabitants" to be admitted which would confine the stipulated privileges to citizens alone, the difficulty is diminished only, not removed. The very improper power would still be retained by each state of naturalizing aliens in every other state. In one state residence for a short term confers all the rights of citizenship; in another, qualifications of greater importance are required. An alien, therefore, legally incapacitated for certain rights in the latter, may, by previous residence only in the former, elude his incapacity; and thus the law of one state be preposterously rendered paramount to the law of another, within the jurisdiction of the other. We owe it to mere casualty that very serious embarrassments on this subject have been hitherto escaped. By the laws of several states, certain descriptions of aliens, who had rendered themselves obnoxious, were laid under interdicts inconsistent not only with the rights of citizenship but with the privileges of residence. What would have been the consequence if such persons, by residence or otherwise, had acquired the character of citizens under the laws of another state, and then asserted their rights as such, both to residence and citizenship, within the state proscribing them ? Whatever the legal consequences might have been, other consequences would probably have resulted of too serious a nature not to be provided against. The new Constitution has accordingly, with great propriety, made provision against them, and all others proceeding from the defect of the Confederation on this head, by authorizing the general government to establish an uniform rule of naturalization throughout the United States.

The power of establishing uniform laws of bankruptcy is so intimately connected with the regulation of commerce, and will prevent so many frauds where the parties or their property may lie or be removed into different states, that the expediency of it seems not likely to be drawn into question.

The power of prescribing by general laws the manner in which the public acts, records, and judicial proceedings of each state shall be proved, and the effect they shall have in other states, is an evident and valuable improvement on the clause relating to this subject in the Articles of Confederation. The meaning of the latter is extremely indeterminate, and can be of little importance under any interpretation which it will bear. The power here established may be rendered a very convenient instrument of justice, and be particularly beneficial on the borders of contiguous states, where the effects liable to justice may be suddenly and secretly translated, in any stage of the process, within a foreign jurisdiction.

The power of establishing post-roads must, in every view, be a harmless power, and may perhaps, by judicious management, become productive of great public conveniency. Nothing which tends to facilitate the intercourse between the states can be deemed unworthy of the public care. PUBLIUS.

(c) OTHER POWERS

THE SAME VIEW CONTINUED[1]

The *fourth* class comprises the following miscellaneous powers:

1. A power "to promote the progress of science and useful arts, by securing, for a limited time, to authors and inventors, the exclusive right to their respective writings and discoveries."

The utility of this power will scarcely be questioned. The copyright of authors has been solemnly adjudged, in Great Britain, to be a right at common law. The right to useful inventions seems with equal reason to belong to the inventors. The public good fully coincides in both cases with the claims of individuals. The states cannot separately make effectual provision for either of the cases, and most of them have anticipated the decision of this point, by laws passed at the instance of Congress.

2. "To exercise exclusive legislation in all cases whatsoever, over such district (not exceeding ten miles square) as may by cession of particular states, and the acceptance of Congress, become the seat of the government of the United States; and to exercise like authority over all places purchased by the consent of the legislature of the states in which the same shall be, for the erection of forts, magazines, arsenals, dockyards, and other needful buildings."

The indispensable necessity of complete authority at the seat of government carries its own evidence with it. It is a power exercised by every legislature of the Union, I might say of the world, by virtue of its general supremacy. Without it, not only the public authority might be insulted and its proceedings be interrupted with impunity, but a dependence of the members of the general government on the state comprehending the seat of the government, for protection in the exercise of their duty, might bring on the national councils an imputation of awe or influence, equally dishonorable to the government and dissatisfactory to the other members of the Confederacy. This

[1] No. XLIII (XLII). Madison. Independent Journal, January 23, 1788.

consideration has the more weight, as the gradual accumulation of public improvements at the stationary residence of the government would be both too great a public pledge to be left in the hands of a single state, and would create so many obstacles to a removal of the government as still further to abridge its necessary independence. The extent of this federal district is sufficiently circumscribed to satisfy every jealousy of an opposite nature. And as it is to be appropriated to this use with the consent of the state ceding it; as the state will no doubt provide in the compact for the rights and the consent of the citizens inhabiting it; as the inhabitants will find sufficient inducements of interest to become willing parties to the cession; as they will have had their voice in the election of the government which is to exercise authority over them; as a municipal legislature for local purposes, derived from their own suffrages, will of course be allowed them; and as the authority of the legislature of the state, and of the inhabitants of the ceded part of it, to concur in the cession, will be derived from the whole people of the state, in their adoption of the Constitution, every imaginable objection seems to be obviated.

The necessity of a like authority over forts, magazines, etc., established by the general government, is not less evident. The public money expended on such places, and the public property deposited in them, require that they should be exempt from the authority of the particular state. Nor would it be proper for the places on which the security of the entire Union may depend to be in any degree dependent on a particular member of it. All objections and scruples are here also obviated, by requiring the concurrence of the states concerned in every such establishment.

3. " To declare the punishment of treason, but no attainder of treason shall work corruption of blood, or forfeiture, except during the life of the person attainted."

As treason may be committed against the United States, the authority of the United States ought to be enabled to punish it. But as new-fangled and artificial treasons have been the great engines by which violent factions, the natural offspring of free governments, have usually wreaked their alternate malignity on each other, the Convention have, with great judgment, opposed a barrier to this peculiar danger by inserting a constitutional definition of the crime, fixing the proof necessary for conviction of it, and restraining the Congress, even in punishing it, from extending the consequences of guilt beyond the person of its author.

4. " To admit new states into the Union; but no new state shall be formed or erected within the jurisdiction of any other state; nor any state be formed by the junction of two or more states, or parts of states, without the consent of the legislatures of the states concerned, as well as of the Congress."

In the Articles of Confederation, no provision is found on this important subject. Canada was to be admitted of right, on her joining in the measures of the United States; and the other *colonies*, by which were evidently meant the other British colonies, at the discretion of nine states. The eventual establishment of *new states* seems to have been overlooked by the compilers of that instrument. We have seen the inconvenience of this omission, and the assumption of power into which Congress have been led by it. With great propriety, therefore, has the new system supplied the defect. The general precaution, that no new states shall be formed without the concurrence of the federal authority, and that of the states concerned, is consonant to the principles which ought to govern such transactions. The particular precaution against the erection of new states, by the partition of a state without its consent, quiets the jealousy of the larger states; as that of the smaller is quieted by a like precaution, against a junction of states without their consent.

5. " To dispose of and make all needful rules and regulations respecting the territory or other property belonging to the United States, with a proviso that nothing in the Constitution shall be so construed as to prejudice any claims of the United states, as of any particular state."

This is a power of very great importance, and required by

considerations similar to those which show the propriety of the former. The proviso annexed is proper in itself, and was probably rendered absolutely necessary by jealousies and questions concerning the Western territory sufficiently known to the public.

6. "To guarantee to every state in the Union a republican form of government; to protect each of them against invasion; and on application of the legislature, or of the executive (when the legislature cannot be convened) against domestic violence."

In a confederacy founded on republican principles, and composed of republican members, the superintending government ought clearly to possess authority to defend the system against aristocratic or monarchical innovations. The more intimate the nature of such a union may be, the greater interest have the members in the political institutions of each other; and the greater right to insist that the forms of government under which the compact was entered into should be *substantially* maintained. But a right implies a remedy; and where else could the remedy be deposited than where it is deposited by the Constitution? Governments of dissimilar principles and forms have been found less adapted to a federal coalition of any sort than those of a kindred nature. "As the confederate republic of Germany," says Montesquieu, "consists of free cities and petty states, subject to different princes, experience shows us that it is more imperfect than that of Holland and Switzerland." "Greece was undone," he adds, "as soon as the king of Macedon obtained a seat among the Amphictyons." In the latter case, no doubt, the disproportionate force, as well as the monarchical form, of the new confederate, had its share of influence on the events. It may possibly be asked what need there could be of such a precaution, and whether it may not become a pretext for alterations in the state governments, without the concurrence of the states themselves. These questions admit of ready answers. If the interposition of the general government should not be needed, the provision for such an event will be a harmless superfluity only in the Constitution. But who can say what experiments may be produced by the caprice of particular states, by the ambition of enterprising leaders, or by the intrigues and influence of foreign powers? To the second question it may be answered, that if the general government should interpose by virtue of this constitutional authority, it will be, of course, bound to pursue the authority. But the authority extends no farther than to a *guarantee* of a republican form of government, which supposes a preëxisting government of the form which is to be guaranteed. As long, therefore, as the existing republican forms are continued by the states, they are guaranteed by the federal Constitution. Whenever the states may choose to substitute other republican forms, they have a right to do so, and to claim the federal guarantee for the latter. The only restriction imposed on them is, that they shall not exchange republican for anti-republican constitutions: a restriction which, it is presumed, will hardly be considered as a grievance.

A protection against invasion is due from every society to the parts composing it. The latitude of the expression here used seems to secure each state, not only against foreign hostility, but against ambitious or vindictive enterprises of its more powerful neighbors. The history, both of ancient and modern confederacies, proves that the weaker members of the union ought not to be insensible to the policy of this article.

Protection against domestic violence is added with equal propriety. It has been remarked that even among the Swiss cantons, which, properly speaking, are not under one government, provision is made for this object; and the history of that league informs us that mutual aid is frequently claimed and afforded; and as well by the most democratic as the other cantons. A recent and well-known event among ourselves has warned us to be prepared for emergencies of a like nature.

At first view, it might seem not to square with the republican theory, to suppose either that a majority have not the right, or that a minority will have the force, to subvert a government; and consequently that the federal interposition can never be required but when it would be improper. But theoretic reasoning, in this as in most other cases, must be qualified by the lessons of practice. Why may not illicit combinations, for purposes of violence, be formed as well by a majority of a state, especially a small state, as by a majority of a county, or a district of the same state; and if the authority of the state ought, in the latter case, to protect the local magistracy, ought not the federal authority, in the former, to support the state authority? Besides, there are certain parts of the state constitutions which are so interwoven with the federal Constitution, that a violent blow cannot be given to the one without communicating the wound to the other. Insurrections in a state will rarely induce a federal interposition, unless the number concerned in them bear some proportion to the friends of government. It will be much better that the violence in such cases should be repressed by the superintending power than that the majority should be left to maintain their cause by a bloody and obstinate contest. The existence of a right to interpose will generally prevent the necessity of exerting it.

Is it true that force and right are necessarily on the same side in republican governments? May not the minor party possess such a superiority of pecuniary resources, of military talents and experience, or of secret succors from foreign powers, as will render it superior also in an appeal to the sword? May not a more compact and advantageous position turn the scale on the same side, against a superior number, so situated as to be less capable of a prompt and collected exertion of its strength? Nothing can be more chimerical than to imagine that in a trial of actual force, victory may be calculated by the rules which prevail in a census of the inhabitants, or which determine the event of an election! May it not happen, in fine, that the minority of CITIZENS may become a majority of PERSONS, by the accession of alien residents, of a casual concourse of adventurers, or of those whom the constitution of the state has not admitted to the rights of suffrage? I take no notice of an unhappy species of population abounding in some of the states, who, during the calm of regular government, are sunk below the level of men; but who, in the tempestuous scenes of civil violence, may emerge into the human character, and give a superiority of strength to any party with which they may associate themselves.

In cases where it may be doubtful on which side justice lies, what better umpires could be desired by two violent factions, flying to arms and tearing a state to pieces, than the representatives of confederate states not heated by the local flame? To the impartiality of judges they would unite the affection of friends. Happy would it be if such a remedy for its infirmities could be enjoyed by all free governments; if a project equally effectual could be established for the universal peace of mankind!

Should it be asked, what is to be the redress for an insurrection pervading all the states, and comprising a superiority of the entire force, though not a constitutional right, the answer must be, that such a case, as it would be without the compass of human remedies, so it is fortunately not within the compass of human probability; and that it is a sufficient recommendation of the federal Constitution that it diminishes the risk of a calamity for which no possible constitution can provide a cure.

Among the advantages of a confederate republic enumerated by Montesquieu, an important one is, "that should a popular insurrection happen in one of the states, the others are able to quell it. Should abuses creep into one part, they are reformed by those that remain sound."

7. "To consider all debts contracted and engagements entered into, before the adoption of this Constitution, as being no less valid against the United States under this Constitution, than under the Confederation."

This can only be considered as a declaratory proposition; and may have been inserted, among other reasons, for the satisfaction of the foreign creditors of the United States, who cannot be strangers to the pretended doctrine that a change in the political form of civil society has the magical effect of dissolving its moral obligations.

Among the lesser criticisms which have been exercised on the Constitution, it has been remarked that the validity of engagements ought to have been asserted in favor of the United

States, as well as against them; and in the spirit which usually characterizes little critics, the omission has been transformed and magnified into a plot against the national rights. The authors of this discovery may be told, what few others need to be informed of, that as engagements are in their nature reciprocal, an assertion of their validity on one side necessarily involves a validity on the other side; and that as the article is merely declaratory, the establishment of the principle in one case is sufficient for every case. They may be further told that every constitution must limit its precautions to dangers that are not altogether imaginary; and that no real danger can exist that the government would DARE, with, or even without, this constitutional declaration before it, to remit the debts justly due to the public, on the pretext here condemned.

8. "To provide for amendments to be ratified by three fourths of the states, under two exceptions only."

That useful alterations will be suggested by experience could not but be foreseen. It was requisite, therefore, that a mode for introducing them should be provided. The mode preferred by the Convention seems to be stamped with every mark of propriety. It guards equally against that extreme facility which would render the Constitution too mutable, and that extreme difficulty which might perpetuate its discovered faults. It, moreover, equally enables the general and the state governments to originate the amendment of errors, as they may be pointed out by the experience on one side or on the other. The exception in favor of the equality of suffrage in the Senate was probably meant as a palladium to the residuary sovereignty of the states, implied and secured by that principle of representation in one branch of the legislature, and was probably insisted on by the states particularly attached to that equality. The other exception must have been admitted on the same considerations which produced the privilege defended by it.

9. "The ratification of the conventions of nine states shall be sufficient for the establishment of this Constitution between the states ratifying the same."

This article speaks for itself. The express authority of the people alone could give due validity to the Constitution. To have required the unanimous ratification of the thirteen States would have subjected the essential interests of the whole to the caprice or corruption of a single member. It would have marked a want of foresight in the Convention which our own experience would have rendered inexcusable.

Two questions of a very delicate nature present themselves on this occasion: 1. On what principle the Confederation, which stands in the solemn form of a compact among the states, can be superseded without the unanimous consent of the parties to it? 2. What relation is to subsist between the nine or more states ratifying the Constitution, and the remaining few who do not become parties to it?

The first question is answered at once by recurring to the absolute necessity of the case; to the great principle of self-preservation; to the transcendent law of nature and of nature's God, which declares that the safety and happiness of society are the objects at which all political institutions aim, and to which all such institutions must be sacrificed. PERHAPS, also, an answer may be found without searching beyond the principles of the compact itself. It has been heretofore noted among the defects of the Confederation that in many of the states it had received no higher sanction than a mere legislative ratification. The principle of reciprocality seems to require that its obligation on the other states should be reduced to the same standard. A compact between independent sovereigns, founded on acts of legislative authority, can pretend to no higher validity than a league or treaty between the parties. It is an established doctrine on the subject of treaties, that all the articles are mutually conditions of each other; that a breach of any one article is a breach of the whole treaty; and that a breach, committed by either of the parties, absolves the others, and authorizes them, if they please, to pronounce the compact violated and void. Should it unhappily be necessary to appeal to these delicate truths for a justification for dispensing with the consent of particular states to a dissolution of the federal pact, will not the complaining parties find it a difficult task to answer the MULTIPLIED and IMPORTANT infractions with which they may be confronted? The time has been when it was incumbent on us all to veil the ideas which this paragraph exhibits. The scene is now changed, and with it the part which the same motives dictate.

The second question is not less delicate; and the flattering prospect of its being merely hypothetical forbids an overcurious discussion of it. It is one of those cases which must be left to provide for itself. In general, it may be observed, that although no political relation can subsist between the assenting and dissenting states, yet the moral relations will remain uncanceled. The claims of justice, both on one side and on the other, will be in force, and must be fulfilled; the rights of humanity must in all cases be duly and mutually respected; whilst considerations of a common interest, and, above all, the remembrance of the endearing scenes which are past, and the anticipation of a speedy triumph over the obstacles to reunion, will, it is hoped, not urge in vain MODERATION on one side, and PRUDENCE on the other.

PUBLIUS.

THE SAME VIEW CONTINUED AND CONCLUDED [1]

A *fifth* class of provisions in favor of the federal authority consists of the following restrictions on the authority of the several states:

1. "No state shall enter into any treaty, alliance or confederation, grant letters of marque and reprisal, coin money, emit bills of credit, make anything but gold and silver a legal tender in payment of debt, pass any bill of attainder, *ex post facto* law, or law impairing the obligation of contracts, or grant any title of nobility."

The prohibition against treaties, alliances, and confederations makes a part of the existing articles of union; and for reasons which need no explanation is copied into the new Constitution.

[1] No. XLIV (XLIII). Madison. New York Packet, January 25, 1788.

The prohibition of letters of marque is another part of the old system, but is somewhat extended in the new. According to the former, letters of marque could be granted by the states after a declaration of war; according to the latter, these licenses must be obtained, as well during war as previous to its declaration, from the government of the United States. This alteration is fully justified by the advantage of uniformity in all points which relate to foreign powers, and of immediate responsibility to the nation in all those for whose conduct the nation itself is to be responsible.

The right of coining money, which is here taken from the states, was left in their hands by the Confederation, as a concurrent right with that of Congress, under an exception in favor of the exclusive right of Congress to regulate the alloy and value. In this instance, also, the new provision is an improvement on the old. Whilst the alloy and value depended on the general authority, a right of coinage in the particular states could have no other effect than to multiply expensive mints and diversify the forms and weights of the circulating pieces. The latter inconveniency defeats one purpose for which the power was originally submitted to the federal head; and as far as the former might prevent an inconvenient remittance of gold and silver to the central mint for recoinage, the end can be as well attained by local mints established under the general authority.

The extension of the prohibition to bills of credit must give pleasure to every citizen, in proportion to his love of justice and his knowledge of the true springs of public prosperity. The loss which America has sustained since the peace, from the pestilent effects of paper money on the necessary confidence between man and man, on the necessary confidence in the public councils, on the industry and morals of the people and on the character of republican government, constitutes an enormous debt against the states chargeable with this unadvised measure, which must long remain unsatisfied; or rather an accumulation of guilt, which can be expiated no otherwise than by a voluntary sacrifice on the altar of justice of the power which has been the instrument of it. In addition to these persuasive considerations, it may be observed that the same reasons which show the necessity of denying to the states the power of regulating coin, prove with equal force that they ought not to be at liberty to substitute a paper medium in the place of coin. Had every state a right to regulate the value of its coin, there might be as many different currencies as states, and thus the intercourse among them would be impeded; retrospective alterations in its value might be made, and thus the citizens of other states be injured, and animosities be kindled among the states themselves. The subjects of foreign powers might suffer from the same cause, and hence the Union be discredited and embroiled by the indiscretion of a single member. No one of these mischiefs is less incident to a power in the states to emit paper money than to coin gold or silver. The power to make anything but gold and silver a tender in payment of debts is withdrawn from the states, on the same principle with that of striking a paper currency.

Bills of attainder, *ex post facto* laws, and laws impairing the obligation of contracts, are contrary to the first principles of the social compact and to every principle of sound legislation. The two former are expressly prohibited by the declarations prefixed to some of the state constitutions, and all of them are prohibited by the spirit and scope of these fundamental charters. Our own experience has taught us, nevertheless, that additional fences against these dangers ought not to be omitted. Very properly, therefore, have the Convention added this constitutional bulwark in favor of personal security and private rights; and I am much deceived if they have not, in so doing, as faithfully consulted the genuine sentiments as the undoubted interests of their constituents. The sober people of America are weary of the fluctuating policy which has directed the public councils. They have seen with regret and with indignation that sudden changes and legislative interferences, in cases affecting personal rights, become jobs in the hands of enterprising and influential speculators, and snares to the more industrious and less informed part of the community. They have seen, too, that one legislative interference is but the first link of a long chain of repetitions, every subsequent interference being naturally produced by the effects of the preceding. They very rightly infer, therefore, that some thorough reform is wanting, which will banish speculations on public measures, inspire a general prudence and industry, and give a regular course to the business of society. The prohibition with respect to titles of nobility is copied from the Articles of Confederation, and needs no comment.

2. "No state shall, without the consent of the Congress, lay any imposts or duties on imports or exports, except what may be absolutely necessary for executing its inspection laws; and the net proceeds of all duties and imposts laid by any state on imports or exports, shall be for the use of the treasury of the United States; and all such laws shall be subject to the revision and control of the Congress. No state shall, without the consent of Congress, lay any duties of tonnage, keep troops, or ships of war, in time of peace, enter into any agreement or compact with another state, or with a foreign power, or engage in war, unless actually invaded, or in such imminent danger as will not admit of delay."

The restraint on the power of the states over imports and exports is enforced by all the arguments which prove the necessity of submitting the regulation of trade to the federal councils. It is needless, therefore, to remark farther on this head, than that the manner in which the restraint is qualified seems well calculated at once to secure to the states a reasonable discretion in providing for the conveniency of their imports and exports, and to the United States a reasonable check against the abuse of this discretion. The remaining particulars of this clause fall within reasonings which are either so obvious, or have been so fully developed, that they may be passed over without remark.

The *sixth* and last class consists of the several powers and provisions by which efficacy is given to all the rest.

1. Of these the first is the power "to make all laws" which

shall be necessary and proper for carrying into execution the foregoing powers, and all other powers vested by this Constitution in the government of the United States, or in any department or officer thereof."

Few parts of the Constitution have been assailed with more intemperance than this; yet on a fair investigation of it, as has been elsewhere shown, no part can appear more completely invulnerable. Without the *substance* of this power, the whole Constitution would be a dead letter. Those who object to the article, therefore, as a part of the Constitution, can only mean that the *form* of the provision is improper. But have they considered whether a better form could have been substituted?

There are four other possible methods which the Convention might have taken on this subject. They might have copied the second article of the existing Confederation, which would have prohibited the exercise of any power not *expressly* delegated; they might have attempted a positive enumeration of the powers comprehended under the general terms "necessary and proper"; they might have attempted a negative enumeration of them by specifying the powers excepted from the general definition; they might have been altogether silent on the subject, leaving these necessary and proper powers to construction and inference.

Had the Convention taken the first method of adopting the second article of Confederation, it is evident that the new Congress would be continually exposed, as their predecessors have been, to the alternative of construing the term "*expressly*" with so much rigor as to disarm the government of all real authority whatever, or with so much latitude as to destroy altogether the force of the restriction. It would be easy to show, if it were necessary, that no important power delegated by the Articles of Confederation has been or can be executed by Congress without recurring more or less to the doctrine of *construction* or *implication*. As the powers delegated under the new system are more extensive, the government which is to administer it would find itself still more distressed with the alternative of betraying the public interest by doing nothing, or of violating the Constitution by exercising powers indispensably necessary and proper, but, at the same time, not *expressly* granted.

Had the Convention attempted a positive enumeration of the powers necessary and proper for carrying their other powers into effect, the attempt would have involved a complete digest of laws on every subject to which the Constitution relates; accommodated too, not only to the existing state of things, but to all the possible changes which futurity may produce; for in every new application of a general power, the *particular powers*, which are the means of attaining the *object* of the general power, must always necessarily vary with that object, and be often properly varied whilst the object remains the same.

Had they attempted to enumerate the particular powers or means not necessary or proper for carrying the general powers into execution, the task would have been no less chimerical; and would have been liable to this further objection, that every defect in the enumeration would have been equivalent to a positive grant of authority. If, to avoid this consequence, they had attempted a partial enumeration of the exceptions, and described the residue by the general terms, *not necessary or proper*, it must have happened that the enumeration would comprehend a few of the excepted powers only; that these would be such as would be least likely to be assumed or tolerated, because the enumeration would of course select such as would be least necessary or proper; and that the unnecessary and improper powers included in the residuum would be less forcibly excepted than if no partial enumeration had been made.

Had the Constitution been silent on this head, there can be no doubt that all the particular powers requisite as means of executing the general powers would have resulted to the government, by unavoidable implication. No axiom is more clearly established in law, or in reason, than that wherever the end is required, the means are authorized; wherever a general power to do a thing is given, every particular power necessary for doing it is included. Had this last method, therefore, been pursued by the Convention, every objection now urged against their plan would remain in all its plausibility; and the real inconveniency would be incurred of not removing a pretext which may be seized on critical occasions for drawing into question the essential powers of the Union.

If it be asked what is to be the consequence, in case the Congress shall misconstrue this part of the Constitution, and exercise powers not warranted by its true meaning, I answer, the same as if they should misconstrue or enlarge any other power vested in them; as if the general power had been reduced to particulars, and any one of these were to be violated; the same, in short, as if the state legislatures should violate their respective constitutional authorities. In the first instance, the success of the usurpation will depend on the executive and judiciary departments, which are to expound and give effect to the legislative acts; and in the last resort a remedy must be obtained from the people, who can, by the election of more faithful representatives, annul the acts of the usurpers. The truth is that this ultimate redress may be more confided in against unconstitutional acts of the federal than of the state legislatures, for this plain reason, that as every such act of the former will be an invasion of the rights of the latter, these will be ever ready to mark the innovation, to sound the alarm to the people, and to exert their local influence in effecting a change of federal representatives. There being no such intermediate body between the state legislatures and the people interested in watching the conduct of the former, violations of the state constitutions are more likely to remain unnoticed and unredressed.

2. "This Constitution, and the laws of the United States which shall be made in pursuance thereof; and all treaties made, or which shall be made, under the authority of the United States, shall be the supreme law of the land; and the judges in every

state shall be bound thereby, any thing in the Constitution or laws of any state to the contrary notwithstanding."

The indiscreet zeal of the adversaries to the Constitution has betrayed them into an attack on this part of it also, without which it would have been evidently and radically defective. To be fully sensible of this, we need only suppose for a moment that the supremacy of the state constitutions had been left complete by a saving clause in their favor.

In the first place, as these constitutions invest the state legislatures with absolute sovereignty, in all cases not excepted by the existing Articles of Confederation, all the authorities contained in the proposed Constitution, so far as they exceed those enumerated in the Confederation, would have been annulled, and the new Congress would have been reduced to the same impotent condition with their predecessors.

In the next place, as the constitutions of some of the states do not even expressly and fully recognize the existing powers of the Confederacy, an express saving of the supremacy of the former would, in such states, have brought into question every power contained in the proposed Constitution.

In the third place, as the constitutions of the states differ much from each other, it might happen that a treaty or national law, of great and equal importance to the states, would interfere with some and not with other constitutions, and would consequently be valid in some of the states, at the same time that it would have no effect in others.

In fine, the world would have seen, for the first time, a system of government founded on an inversion of the fundamental principles of all government; it would have seen the authority of the whole society everywhere subordinate to the authority of the parts; it would have seen a monster in which the head was under the direction of the members.

3. "The senators and representatives before mentioned, and the members of the several state legislatures and all executive and judicial officers, both of the United States and of the

several states, shall be bound by oath or affirmation to support this Constitution."

It has been asked why it was thought necessary that the state magistracy should be bound to support the federal Constitution, and unnecessary that a like oath should be imposed on the officers of the United States, in favor of the state constitutions.

Several reasons might be assigned for the distinctions. I content myself with one which is obvious and conclusive. The members of the federal government will have no agency in carrying the state constitutions into effect. The members and officers of the state governments, on the contrary, will have an essential agency in giving effect to the federal Constitution. The election of the President and Senate will depend, in all cases, on the legislatures of the several states. And the election of the House of Representatives will equally depend on the same authority in the first instance; and will, probably, forever be conducted by the officers, and according to the laws, of the states.

4. Among the provisions for giving efficacy to the federal powers might be added those which belong to the executive and judiciary departments; but as these are reserved for particular examination in another place, I pass them over in this.

We have now reviewed, in detail, all the articles composing the sum or quantity of power delegated by the proposed Constitution to the federal government, and are brought to this undeniable conclusion, that no part of the power is unnecessary or improper for accomplishing the necessary objects of the Union. The question, therefore, whether this amount of power shall be granted or not, resolves itself into another question, whether or not a government commensurate to the exigencies of the Union shall be established; or, in other words, whether the Union itself shall be preserved. PUBLIUS.

(*d*) THE POWERS OF THE FEDERAL AND THE STATE GOVERNMENTS COMPARED

A further Discussion of the supposed Danger from the Powers of the Union, to the State Governments[1]

Having shown that no one of the powers transferred to the federal government is unnecessary or improper, the next question to be considered is, whether the whole mass of them will be dangerous to the portion of authority left in the several states.

The adversaries to the plan of the Convention, instead of considering in the first place what degree of power was absolutely necessary for the purposes of the federal government, have exhausted themselves in a secondary inquiry into the possible consequences of the proposed degree of power to the governments of the particular states. But if the Union, as has been shown, be essential to the security of the people of America against foreign danger; if it be essential to their security against contentions and wars among the different states; if it be essential to guard them against those violent and oppressive factions which embitter the blessings of liberty, and against those military establishments which must gradually poison its very fountain; if, in a word, the Union be essential to the happiness of the people of America, is it not preposterous to urge as an objection to a government, without which the objects of the Union cannot be attained, that such a government may derogate from the importance of the governments of the individual states? Was, then, the American Revolution effected, was the American Confederacy formed, was the precious blood of thousands spilt, and the hard-earned substance of millions lavished, not that the people of America should enjoy peace, liberty, and safety, but that the governments of the individual states, that particular municipal establishments, might enjoy a certain extent of power, and be arrayed with certain dignities and attributes of sovereignty? We have heard of the impious doctrine in the Old World, that the people were made for kings, not kings for the

[1] No. XLV (XLIV). Madison. New York Packet, January 25, 1788.

people. Is the same doctrine to be revived in the New in another shape — that the solid happiness of the people is to be sacrificed to the views of political institutions of a different form? It is too early for politicians to presume on our forgetting that the public good, the real welfare of the great body of the people, is the supreme object to be pursued; and that no form of government whatever has any other value than as it may be fitted for the attainment of this object. Were the plan of the Convention adverse to the public happiness, my voice would be, Reject the plan. Were the Union itself inconsistent with the public happiness, it would be, Abolish the Union. In like manner, as far as the sovereignty of the states cannot be reconciled to the happiness of the people, the voice of every good citizen must be, Let the former be sacrificed to the latter. How far the sacrifice is necessary, has been shown. How far the unsacrificed residue will be endangered, is the question before us.

Several important considerations have been touched in the course of these papers, which discountenance the supposition that the operation of the federal government will by degrees prove fatal to the state governments. The more I revolve the subject, the more fully I am persuaded that the balance is much more likely to be disturbed by the preponderancy of the last than of the first scale.

We have seen, in all the examples of ancient and modern confederacies, the strongest tendency continually betraying itself in the members to despoil the general government of its authorities with a very ineffectual capacity in the latter to defend itself against the encroachments. Although, in most of these examples, the system has been so dissimilar from that under consideration as greatly to weaken any inference concerning the latter from the fate of the former, yet, as the states will retain, under the proposed Constitution, a very extensive portion of active sovereignty, the inference ought not to be wholly disregarded. In the Achæan League it is probable that the federal head had a degree and species of power which gave it a considerable likeness to the government framed by the Convention.

The Lycian Confederacy, as far as its principles and form are transmitted, must have borne a still greater analogy to it. Yet history does not inform us that either of them ever degenerated, or tended to degenerate, into one consolidated government. On the contrary, we know that the ruin of one of them proceeded from the incapacity of the federal authority to prevent the dissensions, and finally the disunion, of the subordinate authorities. These cases are the more worthy of our attention, as the external causes by which the component parts were pressed together were much more numerous and powerful than in our case; and consequently less powerful ligaments within would be sufficient to bind the members to the head, and to each other.

In the feudal system, we have seen a similar propensity exemplified. Notwithstanding the want of proper sympathy in every instance between the local sovereigns and the people, and the sympathy in some instances between the general sovereign and the latter, it usually happened that the local sovereigns prevailed in the rival ship for encroachments. Had no external dangers enforced internal harmony and subordination, and, particularly, had the local sovereigns possessed the affections of the people, the great kingdoms in Europe would at this time consist of as many independent princes as there were formerly feudatory barons.

The state governments will have the advantage of the federal government, whether we compare them in respect to the immediate dependence of the one on the other; to the weight of personal influence which each side will possess; to the powers respectively vested in them; to the predilection and probable support of the people; to the disposition and faculty of resisting and frustrating the measures of each other.

The state governments may be regarded as constituent and essential parts of the federal government, whilst the latter is nowise essential to the operation or organization of the former. Without the intervention of the state legislatures, the President of the United States cannot be elected at all. They must in all cases have a great share in his appointment, and will, perhaps, in most cases, of themselves determine it. The Senate will be elected absolutely and exclusively by the state legislatures. Even the House of Representatives, though drawn immediately from the people, will be chosen very much under the influence of that class of men, whose influence over the people obtains for themselves an election into the state legislatures. Thus, each of the principal branches of the federal government will owe its existence more or less to the favor of the state governments, and must consequently feel a dependence, which is much more likely to beget a disposition too obsequious than too overbearing towards them. On the other side, the component parts of the state governments will in no instance be indebted for their appointment to the direct agency of the federal government, and very little, if at all, to the local influence of its members.

The number of individuals employed under the Constitution of the United States will be much smaller than the number employed under the particular states. There will consequently be less of personal influence on the side of the former than of the latter. The members of the legislative, executive, and judiciary departments of thirteen and more states, the justices of peace, officers of militia, ministerial officers of justice, with all the county, corporation, and town officers, for three millions and more of people, intermixed, and having particular acquaintance with every class and circle of people, must exceed, beyond all proportion, both in number and influence, those of every description who will be employed in the administration of the federal system. Compare the members of the three great departments of the thirteen states, excluding from the judiciary department the justices of peace, with the members of the corresponding departments of the single government of the Union; compare the militia officers of three millions of people with the military and marine officers of any establishment which is within the compass of probability, or, I may add, of possibility, and in this view alone, we may pronounce the advantage of the states to be decisive. If the federal government is to have collectors of revenue, the state governments will have theirs also.

And as those of the former will be principally on the seacoast, and not very numerous, whilst those of the latter will be spread over the face of the country, and will be very numerous, the advantage in this view also lies on the same side. It is true that the Confederacy is to possess, and may exercise, the power of collecting internal as well as external taxes throughout the states; but it is probable that this power will not be resorted to except for supplemental purposes of revenue; that an option will then be given to the states to supply their quotas by previous collections of their own; and that the eventual collection, under the immediate authority of the Union, will generally be made by the officers, and according to the rules, appointed by the several states. Indeed it is extremely probable that in other instances, particularly in the organization of the judicial power, the officers of the states will be clothed with the correspondent authority of the Union. Should it happen, however, that separate collectors of internal revenue should be appointed under the federal government, the influence of the whole number would not bear a comparison with that of the multitude of state officers in the opposite scale. Within every district to which a federal collector would be allotted, there would not be less than thirty or forty, or even more, officers of different descriptions, and many of them persons of character and weight, whose influence would lie on the side of the state.

The powers delegated by the proposed Constitution to the federal government are few and defined. Those which are to remain in the state governments are numerous and indefinite. The former will be exercised principally on external objects, as war, peace, negotiation, and foreign commerce, with which last the power of taxation will, for the most part, be connected. The powers reserved to the several states will extend to all the objects which, in the ordinary course of affairs, concern the lives, liberties, and properties of the people, and the internal order, improvement, and prosperity of the state.

The operations of the federal government will be most extensive and important in times of war and danger; those of the state governments, in times of peace and security. As the former periods will probably bear a small proportion to the latter, the state governments will here enjoy another advantage over the federal government. The more adequate, indeed, the federal powers may be rendered to the national defense, the less frequent will be those scenes of danger which might favor their ascendancy over the governments of the particular states.

If the new Constitution be examined with accuracy and candor, it will be found that the change which it proposes consists much less in the addition of NEW POWERS to the Union, than in the invigoration of its ORIGINAL POWERS. The regulation of commerce, it is true, is a new power; but that seems to be an addition which few oppose, and from which no apprehensions are entertained. The powers relating to war and peace, armies and fleets, treaties and finance, with the other more considerable powers, are all vested in the existing Congress by the Articles of Confederation. The proposed change does not enlarge these powers; it only substitutes a more effectual mode of administering them. The change relating to taxation may be regarded as the most important; and yet the present Congress have as complete authority to REQUIRE of the states indefinite supplies of money for the common defense and general welfare as the future Congress will have to require them of individual citizens; and the latter will be no more bound than the states themselves have been to pay the quotas respectively taxed on them. Had the states complied punctually with the Articles of Confederation, or could their compliance have been enforced by as peaceable means as may be used with success towards single persons, our past experience is very far from countenancing an opinion that the state governments would have lost their constitutional powers, and have gradually undergone an entire consolidation. To maintain that such an event would have ensued, would be to say at once that the existence of the state governments is incompatible with any system whatever that accomplishes the essential purposes of the Union. PUBLIUS.

The Subject of the Last Paper resumed; with an Examination of the Comparative Means of Influence of the Federal and State Governments[1]

Resuming the subject of the last paper, I proceed to inquire whether the federal government or the state governments will have the advantage with regard to the predilection and support of the people. Notwithstanding the different modes in which they are appointed, we must consider both of them as substantially dependent on the great body of the citizens of the United States. I assume this position here as it respects the first, reserving the proofs for another place. The federal and state governments are in fact but different agents and trustees of the people, instituted with different powers and designated for different purposes. The adversaries of the Constitution seem to have lost sight of the people altogether in their reasonings on this subject; and to have viewed these different establishments, not only as mutual rivals and enemies, but as uncontrolled by any common superior in their efforts to usurp the authorities of each other. These gentlemen must here be reminded of their error. They must be told that the ultimate authority, wherever the derivative may be found, resides in the people alone, and that it will not depend merely on the comparative ambition or address of the different governments, whether either, or which of them, will be able to enlarge its sphere of jurisdiction at the expense of the other. Truth, no less than decency, requires that the event in every case should be supposed to depend on the sentiments and sanction of their common constituents.

Many considerations, besides those suggested on a former occasion, seem to place it beyond doubt that the first and most natural attachment of the people will be to the governments of their respective states. Into the administration of these a greater number of individuals will expect to rise. From the gift of these a greater number of offices and emoluments will

[1] No. XLVI (XLV). Madison. New York Packet, January 29, 1788.

flow. By the superintending care of these, all the more domestic and personal interests of the people will be regulated and provided for. With the affairs of these, the people will be more familiarly and minutely conversant. And with the members of these will a greater proportion of the people have the ties of personal acquaintance and friendship, and of family and party attachments; on the side of these, therefore, the popular bias may well be expected most strongly to incline.

Experience speaks the same language in this case. The federal administration, though hitherto very defective in comparison with what may be hoped under a better system, had, during the war, and particularly whilst the independent fund of paper emissions was in credit, an activity and importance as great as it can well have in any future circumstances whatever. It was engaged, too, in a course of measures which had for their object the protection of everything that was dear, and the acquisition of everything that could be desirable to the people at large. It was, nevertheless, invariably found, after the transient enthusiasm for the early congresses was over, that the attention and attachment of the people were turned anew to their own particular governments; that the federal council was at no time the idol of popular favor; and that opposition to proposed enlargements of its powers and importance was the side usually taken by the men who wished to build their political consequence on the prepossessions of their fellow-citizens.

If, therefore, as has been elsewhere remarked, the people should in future become more partial to the federal than to the state governments, the change can only result from such manifest and irresistible proofs of a better administration as will overcome all their antecedent propensities. And in that case, the people ought not surely to be precluded from giving most of their confidence where they may discover it to be most due; but even in that case the state governments could have little to apprehend, because it is only within a certain sphere that the federal power can, in the nature of things, be advantageously administered.

The remaining points on which I proposed to compare the federal and state governments, are the disposition and the faculty they may respectively possess to resist and frustrate the measures of each other.

It has been already proved that the members of the federal will be more dependent on the members of the state governments than the latter will be on the former. It has appeared also that the prepossessions of the people, on whom both will depend, will be more on the side of the state governments than of the federal government. So far as the disposition of each towards the other may be influenced by these causes, the state governments must clearly have the advantage. But in a distinct and very important point of view, the advantage will lie on the same side. The prepossessions, which the members themselves will carry into the federal government, will generally be favorable to the states; whilst it will rarely happen that the members of the state governments will carry into the public councils a bias in favor of the general government. A local spirit will infallibly prevail much more in the members of the Congress than a national spirit will prevail in the legislatures of the particular states. Every one knows that a great proportion of the errors committed by the state legislatures proceeds from the disposition of the members to sacrifice the comprehensive and permanent interests of the state to the particular and separate views of the counties or districts in which they reside. And if they do not sufficiently enlarge their policy to embrace the collective welfare of their particular state, how can it be imagined that they will make the aggregate prosperity of the Union, and the dignity and respectability of its government, the objects of their affections and consultations? For the same reason that the members of the state legislatures will be unlikely to attach themselves sufficiently to national objects, the members of the federal legislature will be likely to attach themselves too much to local objects. The states will be to the latter what counties and towns are to the former. Measures will too often be decided according to their probable effect, not on the national prosperity and happiness, but on the prejudices, interests, and pursuits of the governments and people of the individual states. What is the spirit that has in general characterized the proceedings of Congress? A perusal of their journals, as well as the candid acknowledgments of such as have had a seat in that assembly, will inform us that the members have but too frequently displayed the character, rather of partisans of their respective states than of impartial guardians of a common interest; that where on one occasion improper sacrifices have been made of local considerations, to the aggrandizement of the federal government, the great interests of the nation have suffered on an hundred, from an undue attention to the local prejudices, interests, and views of the particular states. I mean not by these reflections to insinuate that the new federal government will not embrace a more enlarged plan of policy than the existing government may have pursued, much less, that its views will be as confined as those of the state legislatures; but only that it will partake sufficiently of the spirit of both to be disinclined to invade the rights of the individual states, or the prerogatives of their governments. The motives on the part of the state governments, to augment their prerogatives by defalcations from the federal government, will be overruled by no reciprocal predispositions in the members.

Were it admitted, however, that the federal government may feel an equal disposition with the state governments to extend its power beyond the due limits, the latter would still have the advantage in the means of defeating such encroachments. If an act of a particular state, though unfriendly to the national government, be generally popular in that state, and should not too grossly violate the oaths of the state officers, it is executed immediately and, of course, by means on the spot and depending on the state alone. The opposition of the federal government, or the interposition of federal officers, would but inflame the zeal of all parties on the side of the state, and the evil could not be prevented or repaired, if at all, without the employment of means which must always be resorted to with reluctance and difficulty. On the other hand, should an unwarrantable measure of the federal government be unpopular in particular states, which would seldom fail to be the case, or even a warrantable measure be so, which may sometimes be the case, the means of opposition to it are powerful and at hand. The disquietude of the people; their repugnance and, perhaps, refusal to coöperate with the officers of the Union; the frowns of the executive magistracy of the state; the embarrassments created by legislative devices, which would often be added on such occasions, would oppose, in any state, difficulties not to be despised; would form, in a large state, very serious impediments; and where the sentiments of several adjoining states happened to be in unison, would present obstructions which the federal government would hardly be willing to encounter.

But ambitious encroachments of the federal government, on the authority of the state governments, would not excite the opposition of a single state, or of a few states only. They would be signals of general alarm. Every government would espouse the common cause. A correspondence would be opened. Plans of resistance would be concerted. One spirit would animate and conduct the whole. The same combination, in short, would result from an apprehension of the federal, as was produced by the dread of a foreign yoke; and unless the projected innovations should be voluntarily renounced, the same appeal to a trial of force would be made in the one case as was made in the other. But what degree of madness could ever drive the federal government to such an extremity? In the contest with Great Britain, one part of the empire was employed against the other. The more numerous part invaded the rights of the less numerous part. The attempt was unjust and unwise; but it was not in speculation absolutely chimerical. But what would be the contest in the case we are supposing? Who would be the parties? A few representatives of the people would be opposed to the people themselves; or rather one set of representatives would be contending against thirteen sets of representatives, with the whole body of their common constituents on the side of the latter.

The only refuge left for those who prophesy the downfall of the state governments is the visionary supposition that the federal government may previously accumulate a military force for the projects of ambition. The reasonings contained in these papers must have been employed to little purpose indeed, if it could be necessary now to disprove the reality of this danger. That the people and the states should, for a sufficient period of time, elect an uninterrupted succession of men ready to betray both: that the traitors should, throughout this period, uniformly and systematically pursue some fixed plan for the extension of the military establishment; that the governments and the people of the states should silently and patiently behold the gathering storm, and continue to supply the materials, until it should be prepared to burst on their own heads, must appear to every one more like the incoherent dreams of a delirious jealousy, or the misjudged exaggerations of a counterfeit zeal, than like the sober apprehensions of genuine patriotism. Extravagant as the supposition is, let it however be made. Let a regular army, fully equal to the resources of the country, be formed; and let it be entirely at the devotion of the federal government; still it would not be going too far to say that the state governments, with the people on their side, would be able to repel the danger. The highest number to which, according to the best computation, a standing army can be carried in any country, does not exceed one hundreth part of the whole number of souls, or one twenty-fifth part of the number able to bear arms. This proportion would not yield, in the United States, an army of more than twenty-five or thirty thousand men. To these would be opposed a militia amounting to near half a million of citizens with arms in their hands, officered by men chosen from among themselves, fighting for their common liberties, and united and conducted by governments possessing their affections and confidence. It may well be doubted whether a militia thus circumstanced could ever be conquered by such a proportion of regular troops. Those who are best acquainted with the late successful resistance of this country against the British arms will be most inclined to deny the possibility of it. Besides the advantage of being armed, which the Americans possess over the people of almost every other nation, the existence of subordinate governments, to which the people are attached, and by which the militia officers are appointed, forms a barrier against the enterprises of ambition more insurmountable than any which a simple government of any form can admit of. Notwithstanding the military establishments in the several kingdoms of Europe, which are carried as far as the public resources will bear, the governments are afraid to trust the people with arms. And it is not certain that with this aid alone they would not be able to shake off their yokes. But were the people to possess the additional advantages of local governments chosen by themselves, who could collect the national will and direct the national force, and of officers appointed out of the militia, by these governments, and attached both to them and to the militia, it may be affirmed with the greatest assurance that the throne of every tyranny in Europe would be speedily overturned in spite of the legions which surround it. Let us not insult the free and gallant citizens of America with the suspicion, that they would be less able to defend the rights of which they would be in actual possession than the debased subjects of arbitrary power would be to rescue theirs from the hands of their oppressors. Let us rather no longer insult them with the supposition that they can ever reduce themselves to the necessity of making the experiment, by a blind and tame submission to the long train of insidious measures which must precede and produce it.

The argument under the present head may be put into a very concise form, which appears altogether conclusive. Either the mode in which the federal government is to be constructed will render it sufficiently dependent on the people, or it will not. On the first supposition, it will be restrained by that dependence from forming schemes obnoxious to their constituents.

On the other supposition, it will not possess the confidence of the people, and its schemes of usurpation will be easily defeated by the state governments, who will be supported by the people.

On summing up the considerations stated in this and the last paper, they seem to amount to the most convincing evidence, that the powers proposed to be lodged in the federal government are as little formidable to those reserved to the individual states as they are indispensably necessary to accomplish the purposes of the Union; and that all those alarms which have been sounded, of a meditated and consequential annihilation of the state governments, must, on the most favorable interpretation, be ascribed to the chimerical fears of the authors of them.

PUBLIUS.

VII

THE SYSTEM OF CHECKS AND BALANCES

(a) AN EXAMINATION OF MONTESQUIEU'S DOCTRINE

The Meaning of the Maxim, which requires a Separation of the Departments of Power, examined and ascertained[1]

Having reviewed the general form of the proposed government and the general mass of power allotted to it, I proceed to examine the particular structure of this government, and the distribution of this mass of power among its constituent parts.

One of the principal objections inculcated by the more respectable adversaries to the Constitution is its supposed violation of the political maxim, that the legislative, executive, and judiciary departments ought to be separate and distinct. In the structure of the federal government, no regard, it is said, seems to have been paid to this essential precaution in favor of liberty. The several departments of power are distributed and blended in such a manner as at once to destroy all symmetry and beauty of form, and to expose some of the essential parts of the edifice to the danger of being crushed by the disproportionate weight of other parts.

No political truth is certainly of greater intrinsic value, or is stamped with the authority of more enlightened patrons of liberty, than that on which the objection is founded. The accumulation of all powers, legislative, executive, and judiciary, in the same hands, whether of one, a few, or many, and whether hereditary, self-appointed, or elective, may justly be pronounced the very definition of tyranny. Were the federal Constitution, therefore, really chargeable with this accumulation of power, or with a mixture of powers, having a dangerous tendency to such an accumulation, no further arguments would

[1] No. XLVII (XLVI). Madison. Independent Journal, January 30, 1788.

be necessary to inspire a universal reprobation of the system. I persuade myself, however, that it will be made apparent to every one that the charge cannot be supported, and that the maxim on which it relies has been totally misconceived and misapplied. In order to form correct ideas on this important subject, it will be proper to investigate the sense in which the preservation of liberty requires that the three great departments of power should be separate and distinct.

The oracle who is always consulted and cited on this subject is the celebrated Montesquieu. If he be not the author of this invaluable precept in the science of politics, he has the merit at least of displaying and recommending it most effectually to the attention of mankind. Let us endeavor, in the first place, to ascertain his meaning on this point.

The British Constitution was to Montesquieu what Homer has been to the didactic writers on epic poetry. As the latter have considered the work of the immortal bard as the perfect model from which the principles and rules of the epic art were to be drawn, and by which all similar works were to be judged, so this great political critic appears to have viewed the Constitution of England as the standard, or to use his own expression, as the mirror of political liberty; and to have delivered, in the form of elementary truths, the several characteristic principles of that particular system. That we may be sure, then, not to mistake his meaning in this case, let us recur to the source from which the maxim was drawn.

On the slightest view of the British Constitution, we must perceive that the legislative, executive, and judiciary departments are by no means totally separate and distinct from each other. The executive magistrate forms an integral part of the legislative authority. He alone has the prerogative of making treaties with foreign sovereigns, which, when made, have, under certain limitations, the force of legislative acts. All the members of the judiciary department are appointed by him, can be removed by him on the address of the two Houses of Parliament, and form, when he pleases to consult them, one of his constitutional councils. One branch of the legislative department forms also a great constitutional council to the executive chief, as, on another hand, it is the sole depositary of judicial power in cases of impeachment, and is invested with the supreme appellate jurisdiction in all other cases. The judges, again, are so far connected with the legislative department as often to attend and participate in its deliberations, though not admitted to a legislative vote.

From these facts, by which Montesquieu was guided, it may clearly be inferred that, in saying "There can be no liberty where the legislative and executive powers are united in the same person, or body of magistrates," or, "if the power of judging be not separated from the legislative and executive powers," he did not mean that these departments ought to have no *partial agency* in, or no *control* over, the acts of each other. His meaning, as his own words import, and still more conclusively as illustrated by the example in his eye, can amount to no more than this, that where the *whole* power of one department is exercised by the same hands which possess the *whole* power of another department, the fundamental principles of a free constitution are subverted. This would have been the case in the constitution examined by him, if the king, who is the sole executive magistrate, had possessed also the complete legislative power, or the supreme administration of justice; or if the entire legislative body had possessed the supreme judiciary, or the supreme executive authority. This, however, is not among the vices of that constitution. The magistrate in whom the whole executive power resides cannot of himself make a law, though he can put a negative on every law; nor administer justice in person, though he has the appointment of those who do administer it. The judges can exercise no executive prerogative, though they are shoots from the executive stock; nor any legislative function, though they may be advised with by the legislative councils. The entire legislature can perform no judiciary act, though by the joint act of two of its branches the judges may be removed from their offices, and though one of its branches is possessed of the judicial power in the last resort. The entire legislature, again, can exercise no executive prerogative, though one of its branches constitutes the supreme executive magistracy, and another, on the impeachment of a third, can try and condemn all the subordinate officers in the executive department.

The reasons on which Montesquieu grounds his maxim are a further demonstration of his meaning. "When the legislative and executive powers are united in the same person or body," says he, "there can be no liberty, because apprehensions may arise lest *the same* monarch or senate should *enact* tyrannical laws, to *execute* them in a tyrannical manner." Again: "Were the power of judging joined with the legislative, the life and liberty of the subject would be exposed to arbitrary control, for *the judge* would then be *the legislator*. Were it joined to the executive power, *the judge* might behave with all the violence of *an oppressor*." Some of these reasons are more fully explained in other passages; but briefly stated as they are here, they sufficiently establish the meaning which we have put on this celebrated maxim of this celebrated author.

If we look into the constitutions of the several states, we find that, notwithstanding the emphatical and, in some instances, the unqualified terms in which this axiom has been laid down, there is not a single instance in which the several departments of power have been kept absolutely separate and distinct. New Hampshire, whose constitution was the last formed, seems to have been fully aware of the impossibility and inexpediency of avoiding any mixture whatever of these departments, and has qualified the doctrine by declaring "that the legislative, executive and judiciary powers ought to be kept as separate from, and independent of each other *as the nature of a free government will admit; or as is consistent with that chain of connection, that binds the whole fabric of the constitution in one indissoluble bond of unity and amity.*" Her constitution accordingly mixes these departments in several respects. The senate, which is a branch of the legislative department, is also a judicial tribunal for the trial of impeachments. The president, who is the head of the executive department, is the presiding member also of the senate, and, besides an equal vote in all cases, has a casting vote in case of a tie. The executive head is himself eventually elective every year by the legislative department, and his council is every year chosen by and from the members of the same department. Several of the officers of state are also appointed by the legislature, and the members of the judiciary department are appointed by the executive department.

The constitution of Massachusetts has observed a sufficient though less pointed caution in expressing this fundamental article of liberty. It declares " that the legislative department shall never exercise the executive and judicial powers, or either of them; the executive shall never exercise the legislative and judicial powers, or either of them; the judicial shall never exercise the legislative and executive powers, or either of them." This declaration corresponds precisely with the doctrine of Montesquieu, as it has been explained, and is not in a single point violated by the plan of the Convention. It goes no farther than to prohibit any one of the entire departments from exercising the powers of another department. In the very constitution to which it is prefixed, a partial mixture of powers has been admitted. The executive magistrate has a qualified negative on the legislative body, and the senate, which is a part of the legislature, is a court of impeachment for members both of the executive and judiciary departments. The members of the judiciary department, again, are appointable by the executive department, and removable by the same authority on the address of the two legislative branches. Lastly, a number of the officers of government are annually appointed by the legislative department. As the appointment to offices, particularly executive offices, is in its nature an executive function, the compilers of the constitution have, in this last point at least, violated the rule established by themselves.

I pass over the constitutions of Rhode Island and Connecticut, because they were formed prior to the Revolution, and even before the principle under examination had become an object of political attention.

The constitution of New York contains no declaration on this subject; but appears very clearly to have been framed with an eye to the danger of improperly blending the different departments. It gives, nevertheless, to the executive magistrate a partial control over the legislative department, and, what is more, gives a like control to the judiciary department, and even blends the executive and judiciary departments in the exercise of this control. In its council of appointment, members of the legislative are associated with the executive authority in the appointment of officers, both executive and judiciary. And its court for the trial of impeachments and correction of errors is to consist of one branch of the legislature and the principal members of the judiciary department.

The constitution of New Jersey has blended the different powers of government more than any of the preceding. The governor, who is the executive magistrate, is appointed by the legislature; is chancellor and ordinary or surrogate of the state; is a member of the supreme court of appeals, and president, with a casting vote, of one of the legislative branches. The same legislative branch acts again as executive council of the governor, and with him constitutes the court of appeals. The members of the judiciary department are appointed by the legislative department, and removable by one branch of it on the impeachment of the other.

According to the constitution of Pennsylvania, the president, who is head of the executive department, is annually elected by a vote in which the legislative department predominates. In conjunction with an executive council, he appoints the members of the judiciary department, and forms a court of impeachments for trial of all officers, judiciary as well as executive. The judges of the supreme court and justices of the peace seem also to be removable by the legislature; and the executive power of pardoning in certain cases, to be referred to the same department. The members of the executive council are made ex-officio justices of peace throughout the state.

In Delaware, the chief executive magistrate is annually elected by the legislative department. The speakers of the two legislative branches are vice-presidents in the executive department. The executive chief, with six others, appointed, three by each of the legislative branches, constitute the supreme court of appeals; he is joined with the legislative department in the appointment of the other judges. Throughout the states, it appears that the members of the legislature may at the same time be justices of the peace; in this state, the members of one branch of it are ex-officio justices of the peace, as are also the members of the executive council. The principal officers of the executive department are appointed by the legislative; and one branch of the latter forms a court of impeachments. All officers may be removed on address of the legislature.

Maryland has adopted the maxim in the most unqualified terms; declaring that the legislative, executive, and judicial powers of government ought to be forever separate and distinct from each other. Her constitution, notwithstanding, makes the executive magistrate appointable by the legislative department, and the members of the judiciary by the executive department.

The language of Virginia is still more pointed on this subject. Her constitution declares, " that the legislative, executive and judiciary departments, shall be separate and distinct; so that neither exercise the powers properly belonging to the other; nor shall any person exercise the powers of more than one of them at the same time except that the justices of county courts shall be eligible to either house of assembly." Yet we find not only this express exception, with respect to the members of the inferior courts, but that the chief magistrate, with his executive council, are appointable by the legislature; that two members of the latter are triennially displaced at the pleasure of the legislature; and that all the principal offices, both executive and judiciary, are filled by the same department. The executive prerogative of pardoning, also, is in one case vested in the legislative department.

The constitution of North Carolina, which declares " that the legislative, executive and supreme judicial powers of government, ought to be forever separate and distinct from each other," refers, at the same time, to the legislative department, the appointment not only of the executive chief, but all the principal officers within both that and the judiciary department.

In South Carolina, the constitution makes the executive magistracy eligible by the legislative department. It gives to the latter, also, the appointment of the members of the judiciary department, including even justices of the peace and sheriffs; and the appointment of officers in the executive department down to captains in the army and navy of the state.

In the constitution of Georgia, where it is declared "that the legislative, executive and judiciary departments shall be separate and distinct, so that neither exercise the powers properly belonging to the other," we find that the executive department is to be filled by appointments of the legislature: and the executive prerogative of pardoning to be finally exercised by the same authority. Even justices of the peace are to be appointed by the legislature.

In citing these cases, in which the legislative, executive, and judiciary departments have not been kept totally separate and distinct, I wish not to be regarded as an advocate for the particular organizations of the several state governments. I am fully aware that among the many excellent principles which they exemplify, they carry strong marks of the haste, and still stronger of the inexperience, under which they were framed. It is but too obvious that in some instances the fundamental principle under consideration has been violated by too great a mixture, and even an actual consolidation, of the different powers; and that in no instance has a competent provision been made for maintaining in practice the separation delineated on paper. What I have wished to evince is, that the charge brought against the proposed Constitution, of violating a sacred maxim of free government, is warranted neither by the real meaning annexed to that maxim by its author, nor by the sense in which it has hitherto been understood in America. This interesting subject will be resumed in the ensuing paper.

PUBLIUS.

(b) THE OBJECTION TO A COMPLETE SEPARATION OF POWERS

THE SAME SUBJECT CONTINUED, WITH A VIEW TO THE MEANS OF GIVING EFFICIENCY IN PRACTICE TO THAT MAXIM[1]

It was shown in the last paper that the political apothegm there examined does not require that the legislative, executive, and judiciary departments should be wholly unconnected with each other. I shall undertake, in the next place, to show that unless these departments be so far connected and blended as to give to each a constitutional control over the others, the degree of separation which the maxim requires, as essential to a free government, can never in practice be duly maintained.

It is agreed on all sides that the powers properly belonging to one of the departments ought not to be directly and completely administered by either of the other departments. It is equally evident that neither of them ought to possess, directly or indirectly, an overruling influence over the others, in the administration of their respective powers. It will not be denied that power is of an encroaching nature, and that it ought to be effectually restrained from passing the limits assigned to it. After discriminating, therefore, in theory, the several classes of power, as they may in their nature be legislative, executive, or judiciary, the next and most difficult task is to provide some practical security for each, against the invasion of the others. What this security ought to be is the great problem to be solved.

Will it be sufficient to mark, with precision, the boundaries of these departments, in the constitution of the government, and to trust to these parchment barriers against the encroaching

[1] No. XLVIII (XLVII). Madison. New York Packet, February 1, 1788.

spirit of power? This is the security which appears to have been principally relied on by the compilers of most of the American constitutions. But experience assures us that the efficacy of the provision has been greatly overrated, and that some more adequate defense is indispensably necessary for the more feeble, against the more powerful, members of the government. The legislative department is everywhere extending the sphere of its activity, and drawing all power into its impetuous vortex.

The founders of our republics have so much merit for the wisdom which they have displayed that no task can be less pleasing than that of pointing out the errors into which they have fallen. A respect for truth, however, obliges us to remark that they seem never for a moment to have turned their eyes from the danger to liberty from the overgrown and all-grasping prerogative of an hereditary magistrate, supported and fortified by an hereditary branch of the legislative authority. They seem never to have recollected the danger from legislative usurpations, which, by assembling all power in the same hands, must lead to the same tyranny as is threatened by executive usurpations.

In a government where numerous and extensive prerogatives are placed in the hands of an hereditary monarch, the executive department is very justly regarded as the source of danger, and watched with all the jealousy which a zeal for liberty ought to inspire. In a democracy, where a multitude of people exercise in person the legislative functions, and are continually exposed, by their incapacity for regular deliberation and concerted measures, to the ambitious intrigues of their executive magistrates, tyranny may well be apprehended, on some favorable emergency, to start up in the same quarter. But in a representative republic, where the executive magistracy is carefully limited, both in the extent and the duration of its power; and where the legislative power is exercised by an assembly which is inspired, by a supposed influence over the people, with an intrepid confidence in its own strength; which is sufficiently numerous to feel all the passions which actuate a multitude, yet not so numerous as to be incapable of pursuing the objects of its passions, by means which reason prescribes,—it is against the enterprising ambition of this department that the people ought to indulge all their jealousy and exhaust all their precautions.

The legislative department derives a superiority in our governments from other circumstances. Its constitutional powers being at once more extensive, and less susceptible of precise limits, it can, with the greater facility, mask, under complicated and indirect measures, the encroachments which it makes on the coördinate departments. It is not unfrequently a question of real nicety in legislative bodies, whether the operation of a particular measure will, or will not, extend beyond the legislative sphere. On the other side, the executive power being restrained within a narrower compass, and being more simple in its nature, and the judiciary being described by landmarks still less uncertain, projects of usurpation by either of these departments would immediately betray and defeat themselves. Nor is this all: as the legislative department alone has access to the pockets of the people, and has in some constitutions full discretion, and in all a prevailing influence, over the pecuniary rewards of those who fill the other departments, a dependence is thus created in the latter, which gives still greater facility to encroachments of the former.

I have appealed to our own experience for the truth of what I advance on this subject. Were it necessary to verify this experience by particular proofs, they might be multiplied without end. I might collect vouchers in abundance from the records and archives of every state in the Union. But as a more concise, and at the same time equally satisfactory, evidence, I will refer to the example of two states, attested by two unexceptionable authorities.

The first example is that of Virginia, a state which, as we have seen, has expressly declared in its constitution that the three great departments ought not to be intermixed. The authority in support of it is Mr. Jefferson, who, besides his other advantages for remarking the operation of the government, was himself the chief magistrate of it. In order to convey fully the ideas with which his experience had impressed him on this subject, it will be necessary to quote a passage of some length from his very interesting *Notes on the State of Virginia*, p. 195. "All the powers of government, legislative, executive and judiciary, result to the legislative body. The concentrating these in the same hands is precisely the definition of despotic government. It will be no alleviation, that these powers will be exercised by a plurality of hands, and not by a single one. One hundred and seventy-three despots would surely be as oppressive as one. Let those who doubt it turn their eyes on the republic of Venice. As little will it avail us that they are chosen by ourselves. An *elective despotism* was not the government we fought for; but one which should not only be founded on free principles, but in which the powers of government should be so divided and balanced among several bodies of magistracy, as that no one could transcend their legal limits, without being effectually checked and restrained by the others. For this reason, that convention which passed the ordinance of government laid its foundation on this basis, that the legislative, executive and judiciary departments should be separate and distinct, so that no person should exercise the powers of more than one of them at the same time. *But no barrier was provided between these several powers.* The judiciary and executive members were left dependent on the legislative for their subsistence in office, and some of them for their continuance in it. If, therefore, the legislature assumes executive and judiciary powers, no opposition is likely to be made; nor, if made, can be effectual; because in that case they may put their proceeding into the form of an act of assembly, which will render them obligatory on the other branches. They have accordingly, in *many* instances, *decided rights* which should have been left to *judiciary controversy;* and *the direction of the executive, during the whole time of their session, is becoming habitual and familiar.*"

The other state which I shall have for an example is Pennsylvania: and the other authority, the Council of Censors, which assembled in the years 1783 and 1784. A part of the duty of this body, as marked out by the constitution, was "to inquire whether the constitution had been preserved inviolate in every part, and whether the legislative and executive branches of government had performed their duty as guardians of the people, or assumed to themselves, or exercised, other or greater powers than they are entitled to by the constitution." In the execution of this trust, the council were necessarily led to a comparison of both the legislative and executive proceedings with the constitutional powers of these departments; and from the facts enumerated, and to the truth of most of which both sides in the council subscribed, it appears that the constitution had been flagrantly violated by the legislature in a variety of important instances.

A great number of laws had been passed, violating, without any apparent necessity, the rule requiring that all bills of a public nature shall be previously printed for the consideration of the people; although this is one of the precautions chiefly relied on by the constitution against improper acts of the legislature.

The constitutional trial by jury had been violated, and powers assumed which had not been delegated by the constitution.

Executive powers had been usurped.

The salaries of the judges, which the constitution expressly requires to be fixed, had been occasionally varied; and cases belonging to the judiciary department frequently drawn within legislative cognizance and determination.

Those who wish to see the several particulars falling under each of these heads may consult the journals of the council, which are in print. Some of them, it will be found, may be imputable to peculiar circumstances connected with the war; but the greater part of them may be considered as the spontaneous shoots of an ill-constituted government.

It appears, also, that the executive department had not been innocent of frequent breaches of the constitution. There are three observations, however, which ought to be made on this head: *first*, a great proportion of the instances were either immediately produced by the necessities of the war, or recommended by Congress or the commander-in-chief; *second*, in most of the other instances, they conformed either to the declared or the known sentiments of the legislative department; *third*, the executive department of Pennsylvania is distinguished from that of the other states by the number of members composing it. In this respect it has as much affinity to a legislative assembly as to an executive council. And being at once exempt from the restraint of an individual responsibility for the acts of the body, and deriving confidence from mutual example and joint influence, unauthorized measures would, of course, be more freely hazarded than where the executive department is administered by a single hand, or by a few hands.

The conclusion which I am warranted in drawing from these observations is, that a mere demarcation on parchment of the constitutional limits of the several departments is not a sufficient guard against those encroachments which lead to a tyrannical concentration of all the powers of government in the same hands.

PUBLIUS.

(*c*) SEPARATION OF POWERS NECESSARY TO PREVENT FREQUENT CONSTITUTIONAL AMENDMENTS

THE SAME SUBJECT CONTINUED WITH THE SAME VIEW.[1]

THE author of the *Notes on the State of Virginia*, quoted in the last paper, has subjoined to that valuable work, the draught of a constitution which had been prepared in order to be laid before a convention expected to be called in 1783, by the legislature, for the establishment of a constitution for that commonwealth. The plan, like everything from the same pen, marks a turn of thinking original, comprehensive, and accurate; and is the more worthy of attention, as it equally displays a fervent attachment to republican government, and an enlightened view of the dangerous propensities against which it ought to be guarded. One of the precautions which he proposes, and on

[1] No. XLIX (XLVIII). Madison or Hamilton. Independent Journal, February 2, 1788.

which he appears ultimately to rely as a palladium to the weaker departments of power, against the invasions of the stronger, is perhaps altogether his own, and as it immediately relates to the subject of our present inquiry, ought not to be overlooked.

His proposition is, "that whenever any two of the three branches of government shall concur in opinion, each by the voices of two thirds of their whole number, that a convention is necessary for altering the constitution or *correcting breaches of it*, a convention shall be called for the purpose."

As the people are the only legitimate fountain of power, and it is from them that the constitutional charter, under which the several branches of government hold their power, is derived, it seems strictly consonant to the republican theory, to recur to the same original authority, not only whenever it may be necessary to enlarge, diminish, or new-model the powers of government, but also whenever any one of the departments may commit encroachments on the chartered authorities of the others. The several departments being perfectly coördinate by the terms of their common commission, neither of them, it is evident, can pretend to an exclusive or superior right of settling the boundaries between their respective powers; and how are the encroachments of the stronger to be prevented, or the wrongs of the weaker to be redressed, without an appeal to the people themselves; who, as the grantors of the commission, can alone declare its true meaning and enforce its observance?

There is certainly great force in this reasoning, and it must be allowed to prove, that a constitutional road to the decision of the people ought to be marked out and kept open, for certain great and extraordinary occasions. But there appear to be insuperable objections against the proposed recurrence to the people, as a provision in all cases for keeping the several departments of power within their constitutional limits.

In the first place, the provision does not reach the case of a combination of two of the departments against the third. If the legislative authority, which possesses so many means of operating on the motives of the other departments, should be able to gain to its interest either of the others, or even one third of its members, the remaining department could derive no advantage from this remedial provision. I do not dwell, however, on this objection, because it may be thought to lie rather against the modification of the principle than against the principle itself.

In the next place, it may be considered as an objection inherent in the principle, that as every appeal to the people would carry an implication of some defect in the government, frequent appeals would in great measure deprive the government of that veneration which time bestows on everything, and without which perhaps the wisest and freest governments would not possess the requisite stability. If it be true that all governments rest on opinion, it is no less true that the strength of opinion in each individual, and its practical influence on his conduct, depend much on the number which he supposes to have entertained the same opinion. The reason of man, like man himself, is timid and cautious, when left alone; and acquires firmness and confidence, in proportion to the number with which it is associated. When the examples which fortify opinion are *ancient* as well as *numerous*, they are known to have a double effect. In a nation of philosophers this consideration ought to be disregarded. A reverence for the laws would be sufficiently inculcated by the voice of an enlightened reason. But a nation of philosophers is as little to be expected as the philosophical race of kings wished for by Plato. And in every other nation, the most rational government will not find it a superfluous advantage to have the prejudices of the community on its side.

The danger of disturbing the public tranquillity by interesting too strongly the public passions, is a still more serious objection against a frequent reference of constitutional questions to the decision of the whole society. Notwithstanding the success which has attended the revisions of our established forms of government, and which does so much honor to the virtue and intelligence of the people of America, it must be confessed that the experiments are of too ticklish a nature to be unnecessarily multiplied. We are to recollect that all the existing constitutions were formed in the midst of a danger which repressed the passions most unfriendly to order and concord; of an enthusiastic confidence of the people in their patriotic leaders, which stifled the ordinary diversity of opinions on great national questions; of a universal ardor for new and opposite forms, produced by a universal resentment and indignation against the ancient government; and whilst no spirit of party connected with the changes to be made, or the abuses to be reformed, could mingle its leaven in the operation. The future situations in which we must expect to be usually placed, do not present any equivalent security against the danger which is apprehended.

But the greatest objection of all is that the decisions which would probably result from such appeals would not answer the purpose of maintaining the constitutional equilibrium of the government. We have seen that the tendency of republican governments is to an aggrandizement of the legislative at the expense of the other departments. The appeals to the people, therefore, would usually be made by the executive and judiciary departments. But whether made by one side or the other, would each side enjoy equal advantages on the trial? Let us view their different situations. The members of the executive and judiciary departments are few in number, and can be personally known to a small part only of the people. The latter, by the mode of their appointment, as well as by the nature and permanency of it, are too far removed from the people to share much in their prepossessions. The former are generally the objects of jealousy, and their administration is always liable to be discolored and rendered unpopular. The members of the legislative department, on the other hand, are numerous. They are distributed and dwell among the people at large. Their connections of blood, of friendship, and of acquaintance embrace a great proportion of the most influential part of the society. The nature of their public trust implies a personal influence among the people, and that they are more immediately the confidential guardians of the rights and liberties of the people. With these advantages, it can hardly be supposed that the adverse party would have an equal chance for a favorable issue.

But the legislative party would not only be able to plead their cause most successfully with the people: they would probably be constituted themselves the judges. The same influence which had gained them an election into the legislature would gain them a seat in the convention. If this should not be the case with all, it would probably be the case with many, and pretty certainly with those leading characters on whom everything depends in such bodies. The convention, in short, would be composed chiefly of men who had been, who actually were, or who expected to be, members of the department whose conduct was arraigned. They would consequently be parties to the very question to be decided by them.

It might, however, sometimes happen that appeals would be made under circumstances less adverse to the executive and judiciary departments. The usurpations of the legislature might be so flagrant and so sudden as to admit of no specious coloring. A strong party among themselves might take side with the other branches. The executive power might be in the hands of a peculiar favorite of the people. In such a posture of things, the public decision might be less swayed by prepossessions in favor of the legislative party. But still it could never be expected to turn on the true merits of the question. It would inevitably be connected with the spirit of preëxisting parties, or of parties springing out of the question itself. It would be connected with persons of distinguished character and extensive influence in the community. It would be pronounced by the very men who had been agents in, or opponents of, the measures to which the decision would relate. The *passions*, therefore, not the *reason*, of the public would sit in judgment. But it is the reason of the public alone that ought to control and regulate the government. The passions ought to be controlled and regulated by the government.

We found in the last paper that mere declarations in the written Constitution are not sufficient to restrain the several departments within their legal limits. It appears in this, that occasional appeals to the people would be neither a proper nor an effectual provision for that purpose. How far the provisions of a different nature contained in the plan above quoted might be adequate, I do not examine. Some of them are unquestionably founded on sound political principles, and all of them are framed with singular ingenuity and precision.

PUBLIUS.

Bei Fragen zur Produktsicherheit wenden Sie sich bitte an:
If you have any questions regarding product safety,
please contact:

Walter de Gruyter GmbH
Genthiner Straße 13
10785 Berlin
productsafety@degruyterbrill.com